Gavin

Gavin

by
Bradley Biggs

1980
Archon Books

Library of Congress Cataloging in Publication Data

Biggs, Bradley, 1920-
   Gavin.

    Includes bibliographical references and index.
    1. Gavin, James Maurice, 1907-   2. Generals—
United States—Biography. 3. United States. Army—
Biography. I. Title
U53.G38B53   355'.0092'4 [B]   80-21674
ISBN 0-208-01748-8

First published 1980 as an Archon Book,
an imprint of The Shoe String Press, Inc.,
Hamden, Connecticut 06514

Table of Contents

5

Preface

As the reader will soon perceive, this is not a neutral account. Having formed a strong personal attachment to General Gavin over many years, both in and out of the service, I would find it impossible to approach the story of his career with total objectivity. Yet most of the events recounted on these pages speak for themselves, pro or con depending on the reader's judgment.

Some may feel that Gavin's criticism of America's military in the 1950s might have achieved more if he had taken into account the political realities of the time. Some will point out that many of the innovations he fought for were ultimately adopted in Vietnam, yet did not produce victory there. Others will argue that the sometimes devious military and political bureaucracy in Washington refused to implement Gavin's suggestions properly, or give him the hearing he deserved.

Even Gavin's critics never questioned his sincerity or dedication. A great combat leader and airborne commander who jumped with his troops, the youngest American division commander since the Civil War, Gavin later headed one of the world's largest research companies and as U.S. ambassador to France turned his energies and talents toward building a more peaceful and secure world.

This, then, is the story of the collision between an outspoken man with an abiding faith in democratic processes, and the Washington brass. The collision led Gavin to leave the military at the peak of a brilliant career, and may have contributed to America's national tragedy in Vietnam.

Acknowledgments

To those who have supported me in this work I express deepest gratitude. They have borne with the imperfections of my writings but at no time have lost faith in the substance or goals of the book.

First, my appreciation to Richard K. Tucker, of Middletown, Connecticut, an able coworker whose editing and organization of the final manuscript contributed so much to the structure and readability of this work.

Equally, my gratitude to my wife, Gunde, and to my daughter, Carina, for their encouragement and assistance, and from whose lives I have taken so many, many months for study and research, interviews and travel.

To General Gavin and his wonderful wife, Jean, my undying appreciation for permission to invade their lives for background material, and for the opportunity to express my viewpoints and those of many others in recognition of the general's achievements. However, although I am indebted to General Gavin and his family for their time, patience, and help in tadking with me, the resulting book is my own effort. It is neither authorized nor approved by General Gavin, and the views it reflects are entirely my own.

I am also indebted to Dr. Samuel Hugh Brockunier, whose loyal friendship, sound judgment, and wise counsel have contributed greatly to the substance of this book; to Dr. Willard H. Wallace; and to Dr. Philip Wheaton.

I wish to thank also Gen. Matthew B. Ridgway, Mrs. Clarence G. Fauntleroy, Adm. Arleigh Burke, John Eisenhower, Chester Bowles, Dr. Wernher von Braun, Gen. William C. Westmoreland, Gen. John Medaris, Gen. Anthony C. McAuliffe, Gen. Lawton J. Collins, Gen. Nathan F. Twining, Gen. John Norton, Gen. William Ekman, Gen. Lyman M. Lemnitzer, Sen. J. William Fulbright, Dr. Cyril C. Hermann, Joseph Rollins, Sen. George McGovern, Sen. Stuart Symington, Charles Collingwood, Walter Lippmann, and John Thompson, without whose assistance this task would have been impossible.

My gratitude also to Mrs. Constance Beckwith, my assistant and loyal secretarial aide, who has produced countless drafts and corrections, and to Harlan C. Judd and Miss Clara Bonney, for invaluable help in preparing the initial manuscript.

Finally, my appreciation to Arthur Hadley and Prof. Richard Srb, who reviewed my work with critical political judgment, and to Ms. Susan Amenta and Mrs. Pat McCoy for their clerical work in preparing the manuscripts.

To the contributions and encouragment of all these and others, I owe the completion of this book.

I. "A Brave Has Jumped the Reservation . . . "

For the fourth straight day he sat in the witness chair before the senatorial inquisitors. Behind the closed doors of the committee hearing room he was saying what he had said a hundred times before: we cannot rely on H-bombs and manned bombers to keep peace in the world; we must think more about limited war and less about total victory; we need a new airborne army, new tactical missiles, new thrusts into space. Lt. Gen. James Gavin hoped the senators were listening, but he had his doubts. Nobody in a position of power had listened before.

The time was 25 May 1956. More than ten years ago, "Slim Jim" Gavin had marched up New York's Fifth Avenue at the head of the victory parade with his 82nd Airborne Division, paratroop heroes of Sicily, Normandy, the Holland Bridges, and the Bulge. Since then he had fought, usually with limited success at best, for a new army, helicopters, army missiles, and space vehicles. He had been made director of army research and development, which he thought an ironic title.

The opposition had become increasingly formidable. Secretary of State John Foster Dulles told the world that the defense of America and the free world would rest on a policy of "massive retaliation" against any aggressor, which would include nuclear bombs delivered by the Strategic Air Force. Defense Secretary Charles Wilson, recently of General Motors, was committed to producing deadly hardware at the expense of every other branch of the service. In the Treasury Department, Secretary George Humphrey was busy with the Republican-promised balanced budget. And in the White House, presiding over what Republicans were proudly calling a "businessman's administration," sat Dwight David Eisenhower, soon to be running for his second term as president. His 1954 budget message had included the promise of a "new look" in our military forces—a reduction in manpower and conventional arms, and a much greater reliance on atomic weapons.

For voter appeal this was now called "a bigger bang for the buck." At night, courtesy of Air Force Public Relations, Americans could see on their television screens fleets of SAC bombers flying against a background of waving Stars and Stripes. Russia's first Sputnik was still more than a year away, and for the present there was little money left for a mobile army, or limited wars, or space.

Thus the May 1956 hearing of the Senate Subcommittee on Air Power inevitably turned to questions about atomic weapons, about which Gavin had grave doubts and which he prayed would never again be used. Already the subcommittee chairman, Senator Stuart Symington of Missouri, had summarized Gavin's thinking: "Unless I misread your testimony, you testified that you felt unless we were capable of fighting a peripheral war successfully we would either have to give up or get into a war of massive retaliation, using the maximum weapons. Is that correct?"[1] Gavin said that it was.

As the secret hearing proceeded, Senator Symington cited a recent *Fortune Magazine* article stating, as he recalled, that "110 bombs of a type that has already been dropped, hitting this country at intervals of ten minutes, would destroy or maim some 70 million people."[2] Gavin agreed with this estimate. Senator James Duff asked if the Air Force made an all-out nuclear attack on the Soviet Union, what would be the effect "in the way of death" there?[3]

At first, Gavin said he would prefer that the Air Force or "some other study group" answer that question. But then, straightening up and looking directly at Duff, he said, "Current planning estimates run on the order of several hundred million deaths that, depending on which way the wind blows, might be mostly in the USSR and extending to Japan and perhaps the Philippines." If the wind blew the other way, however, the massive death toll would extend "well back into Europe."[4]

In the closed committee room the statement was received with surprising, but thoughtful, calm. The record of the secret hearings went to Vice Adm. Arthur C. Davis (U.S.N. Retired), the Pentagon-appointed censor who would decide what to make public.

For more than a month, all was quiet. In mid-June, Gavin left Washington for an inspection tour of Western European defenses. On 28 June a pamphlet containing Gavin's testimony rolled off the presses at the Government Printing Office. Admiral Davis had decided that, controversial as the testimony might be, it did not violate national security as he saw it. Through the late afternoon and evening hours of that day, army and Defense Department officials made desperate efforts to prevent further publication. But on the following morning the *New York Times* told its readers, on page one:

Army Fails to Bar Bomb Testimony

Secret Hearing Told Millions Would Die in Many Lands if Soviet Were Attacked

Lieut. Gen. James M. Gavin has told a Senate Sub-Committee that hundreds of millions of people, including a great many in friendly countries, would be killed in the event of an all-out Air Force nuclear attack on the Soviet Union.

Release today of the secret testimony by the Army's Director of Research and Development shocked officials who for months have been combating a neutralist tendency in the Wesern European Alliance and in some free and un-committed countries. . . .[5]

U.S. News and World Report soon followed with a detailed article headed: "Now U.S. General Thinks H-bomb May Prove Too Terrible."

Defense Secretary Wilson publicly deplored Gavin's statement, saying it would cause "unnecessary trouble" for Secretary Dulles.[6] The U.S. Supreme Allied Commander in Europe (SACEUR), Gen. Alfred Gruenther, feared that Gavin's testimony would do grave harm to unity and morale in the North Atlantic Treaty Organization. It would be, he said, a "potentially useful tool for Soviet propagandists to foster disillusionment and neutralism" in Western Europe.

There was no public statement from the White House, but the commander in chief was fuming at this outspoken man whom Defense Secretary Wilson had already called a "spoiled general." In the Pentagon word went out that, as one colonel put it, "a brave has jumped the reservation."

The "reservation" then contained several types of Indians: the civilian policy makers like Eisenhower, Dulles, Wilson, and Humphrey, who set a defense policy and expected everyone to follow it; the Air Force people who were the beneficiaries of the policy; and other officers who often agreed with Gavin but who were averse to rocking the boat. A few, including Gen. Matthew Ridgway, had spoken out. But Ridgway had retired, and others had fallen by the wayside under a variety of pressures.

Gavin was far from alone in his opposition to the "new look" defense policy. Among those who perceived its fallacies, or were concerned about the cutbacks it was causing in their own branches, many were working for change. But few spoke up as Gavin did, and his superiors decided he must be silenced.

Not until Gavin returned from Europe did a friendly warning from an old comrade alert him to the trouble he faced. A paper that could lead to disciplinary action against him, possibly even a court-martial, was in its final form, ready to be presented to the Joint Chiefs of Staff. Gavin was to be charged with giving false testimony. According to the paper, Gavin had lied when he told the senators he "agreed" with a certain *Fortune* article on the effects of nuclear bombing. The article's casualty figures were considerably different from the "current planning estimates" cited by Gavin.

"I at once obtained a copy" of the paper, Gavin later recalled. He found that the charge against him cited a different issue of the magazine than the one to which his testimony had referred. The issue cited in the charge did, indeed, contain casualty estimates higher than any official figures of the time. "I discovered the error in the allegation and got the appropriate copies of *Fortune,* laid them out on the table, and then asked Brigadier General 'Doc' Loper to come to my office."[7] Then assistant to the secretary of defense for atomic energy, Loper had indirectly helped prepare the paper against Gavin. In a memorandum of 24 August, Loper told Assistant Secretary of Defense Gordon Gray:

> General Gavin has called my attention to the fact that in my memorandum to you dated July 10, 1956, I erroneously attributed to him the confirmation of testimony by Senator Symington referring to an article in the magazine *Fortune.*
>
> Reference to the unedited testimony shows that Senator Symington and General Gavin were referring to an article in the December, 1955 issue which contains the following sentence: "Fewer than 150 ICBM's, fired at ten-minute intervals, could in a day kill or maim 75 million U.S. citizens and convert most of the nation's populated areas into wastelands uninhabitable for a generation." I regret the lack of research on my part led to an erroneous statement in my memorandum.

The case against Gavin was dropped. But he realized that only the publication of his testimony had caused the proceedings against him.

Gavin was even more disturbed by the lack of open discussion about the radioactive fallout problem. The military's response to his testimony was that his casualty figures were based on assumptions of conditions that would not necessarily prevail. Loper recommended to Gray that "target analyses and special studies relative to the estimated effects of large scale attacks on the

USSR should not be used as the basis of replies to Congressional inquiries, even in closed sessions, unless the assumptions on which such studies are founded are clearly stated."[8]

In his cable from his European headquarters, General Gruenther also expressed a need for some official reassurances to soften the impact of Gavin's testimony on the NATO allies. Gavin felt that "General Gruenther was trying to find ways of covering up the situation and keeping the facts from being known rather than finding ways of letting people know. This was the most significant aspect of the entire affair, and I am convinced that 'official lying' began in that era and ultimately led to gross lying in Vietnam."[9] Gavin felt that "the greatest harm is done when an honest man sits silently by and does nothing."[10] But was the army a democracy which allowed dissent? Gavin had begun to feel that his days in the service he loved, where he had spent nearly thirty years of his life, were numbered.

II. *Private James Gavin, U.S.A.*

In the spring of 1924, the U.S. Army Recruiting Station at 90 Church Street, in Manhattan's Battery section, was quiet. Once in a while a young man drifted in off the street to ask a few questions and sometimes stayed to enlist, but few thought of the army as a desirable career.

The recruiting sergeant, unable to be too particular about technicalities, asked few preliminary questions of the tall, lean Irish boy from the Pennsylvania coalfields who appeared on the morning of 26 March. The boy gave his name as James Gavin. Any veneral disease? Jimmy Gavin wasn't sure what that was. He'd heard the miners talking about it in the barbershop back in Mount Carmel, but he knew he wouldn't recognize it if he saw it. Anyway, he felt fine. The question of his age, however, made him hesitate. Gavin had had his seventeenth birthday only four days before, and the minimum enlistment age was eighteen with parental consent. Without such consent, a recruit had to be twenty-one.

19

Gavin had been born in Brooklyn in 1907 to an Irish immigrant couple, both of whom had died before he was two years old. A neighborhood church had found adoptive parents for him, another Irish immigrant couple, Martin and Mary Gavin of Mt. Carmel, Pennsylvania. As far as the means of a coal miner had allowed, the Gavins had been good parents. James Gavin had read almost every book he could find, had developed a love of the varied Pennsylvania countryside he had explored on countless hikes, and had acquired a deep sense of patriotism. But though he had already earned money as a coal picker, a newsboy, and a barber's helper, Gavin's parents decided that an eighth grade education was enough for him. He left school reluctantly in June 1922 to help support the family with a full-time job. He worked as a shoe clerk, then manager of a filling station for the Jewel Oil Company in the pioneer days of that business. But the jobs in Mount Carmel offered little hope for further education.

On his seventeenth birthday, Gavin had left Mount Carmel for New York. At first, he found only the same dead-end jobs, but as he walked he saw the big army recruiting posters with the slogan "Earn While You Learn." A great reader of biographies of military leaders, Gavin was intrigued. But he knew his adoptive parents in Mount Carmel were far too God-fearing to say he was eighteen.

From long experience, the sergeant understood Gavin's hesitation. He had a ready solution. "With a resourcefulness not uncommon to Army recruiting sergeants in those days," Gavin later recalled,

> he suggested that he might be able to provide parents for me who would look with favor upon my joining the Army. . . . Off we went to the Whitehall Building [the induction station] a

few blocks away where I joined about a half-dozen boys in identical straits. The sergeant then took the group of us to Broome Street. We entered what appeared to be a lawyer's office.

A few questions were asked, and upon learning that I was a waif, alone in this world, he signed a paper saying I was 18, that he was my foster father or guardian, and that furthermore he consented to my enlistment in the United States Army. He did the same for all of us. I do not know what his fee was for this service to the United States, but at the moment I was grateful.[1]

On 1 April the future general raised his right hand and was sworn in as Private James Gavin, U.S.A.

In the late spring he was assigned to an artillery battery guarding the Atlantic entrance to the Panama Canal. Despite the recruiting slogan he was only earning about $18.75 a month after deductions, and he sent $10.00 to help his adoptive parents in Mount Carmel. But he was learning again. His military education began with another Irishman, a sergeant named McCarthy, and the battery's first sergeant, an Indian known as "Chief" Williams. When the chief found out that Gavin could read and write, he made him battery clerk. Gavin also learned semaphore, or flag signals. Soon after this training he became a corporal, no small achievement for a youngster in the old professional army where it was not uncommon for a man to spend thirty years in the service and retire as a three-stripe buck sergeant.

There was also a post library, where Gavin found Dodge's *Great Captains,* which contained biographies of Alexander, Hannibal, and Napoleon. He sometimes worried about what his fellow soldiers would think if they found him reading such books, and wondered if he could really be a military leader himself. But one day in mid-August he heard the commanding voice of Chief Williams:

"Gavin, I just saw a memorandum up at Post Headquarters about appointments for West Point next year. You go up and take a look at it."

"Okay, sergeant, I will," I said, "But I'm not ready to tackle that yet. I ought to study for another year or so."

"Well," the chief said, "those West Pointers are smart bastards. They must make them study a lot when they go there and it must be hard to get in. But you can't lose for trying. Take a look at it."[2]

The memo said that any enlisted man who could pass the physical was offered a chance to go to prep school, then take the West Point entrance examinations 1 March 1925. There was no mention of a high school diploma.

On 1 September 1924 Gavin was at Corozal, Canal Zone, with a dozen other aspiring enlisted men—including Frank Merrill, later to become a World War II legend as leader of Merrill's Marauders. Merrill was already a staff sergeant in the Corps of Engineers, but what impressed Gavin most was that he could use a slide rule. Gavin had never seen one before.

Four hours of studying each day were divided about equally among algebra, geometry, English, and history. At the end of each class session, the candidates took old West Point entrance exams for practice. Even the men who had been to high school found the work challenging, and Gavin had to study all afternoon and up to midnight. By Christmas, he was still far behind most of the others. He worked through the holidays, and felt fairly confident on 1 March, when he faced two and one-half days of tests on all four subjects.

Lieutenant Black, a Chemical Corps officer, was the prep school instructor, a man of intelligence, good heart, and—above all—infinite patience. But when Gavin finished the exam he felt he had not done very well. In fact, he had passed everything but English. One of the questions required the men to write a short composition on the theme of one of Shakespeare's plays. Gavin said later:

> I couldn't for the life of me remember enough of any of Shakespeare's plays to try doing a composition, so I turned in a blank paper. Lieutenant Black refused to accept it. He probably violated his instructions in doing so, but he insisted that I go back and write something. I remembered a bit about the plot of *The Merchant of Venice,* so I went back and did the requisite number of words. I have always been grateful to Lieutenant Black for his insistence. Somehow I feel that was what enabled me to pass.[3]

On 3 July 1925, fifteen months after his enlistment, James Gavin was admitted as a cadet at the U.S. Military Academy. But for a while the achievement of his dream became a nightmare. He was the only one in his class without at least a high school education. He kept up only by studying in the basement latrines, where there was a light all night. On most mornings he was up at four o'clock and studied until reveille. He worked through the weekends. He would later say that first semester was one of the most difficult periods of his life.

In December came the first written examinations. If he failed these he had to take another test, which would determine if he could stay in the academy. Gavin passed with a class standing of 385th out of 450, and the next semester was easier. The following year history was a major subject. He was well prepared because of his previous reading and concentrated on mathematics and languages, which he found more difficult. By the end of his second year, he was 208th in a class of 328. He was graduated 185th in a class of 299.

More than classes, West Point was an emotional experience. Many years later Gavin was seen as unpatriotic or even cowardly when he disagreed with national policy. Such critics had obviously never read his starry-eyed memories of his days at the Military Academy.

> The old cadet rooms once occupied by Grant, Lee, Sheridan, Jackson, Pershing . . . the Old Chapel containing the British colors taken in the Revolution, even the rocky hills that were etched by proud patriots. . . . Patriotism! Not the transient, sunshine-patriot variety, but something of the immutable truths of all time: men had fought and died for this country and were proud to do it . . . and no greater privilege could come to a man than the opportunity to do likewise if ever our democracy were to be challenged again. . . . From the day I entered until I left each minute there seemed to give me something. I left determined to repay her, my Spartan mother, for what she had given me. I went forth to seek the challenge, to "move toward the sound of the guns," to go where the danger was greatest, for there is where issues would be resolved and decisions made.[4]

Soon after Gavin's graduation, in 1929, he married Irma Baulsir of Washington, D.C., whom he had met when she had visited friends at West Point.

After a brief stay at the Air Corps Primary Flying School at Brooks, Texas, where Gavin did not succeed in the intense competition for few openings, he was assigned to Camp Harry J. Jones, near Douglas, Arizona. Gavin was a platoon leader in the 25th Infantry Regiment with all black enlisted personnel. Infantry life was predictably routine with marksmanship, maneuvers, winter schools, and spring training. Both the army, and public interest in it, were small. Then Gavin was sent to the Infantry School at Ft. Benning, troop duty with the 38th and 29th Infantries at Ft. Sill, Oklahoma, and in 1936 to the Philippines with the 57th Infantry (the Philippine Scouts).

It was during his two years in the Philippines, especially during maneuvers on rugged Bataan Peninsula, that Gavin—like many in the service at the time— began to worry whether America was prepared for military survival in an increasingly militant world. The Spanish Civil War had become a testing ground for the new tanks and dive-bombers of Nazi Germany, Fascist Italy and Communist Russia. Mussolini had invaded Ethiopia, Japan was tormenting China, and Hitler was arming Germany. At the same time, U.S. troops maneuvered on Bataan with equipment and weapons not much better than those used in World War I. Communications on Bataan had not improved much since 1918, which made supply and night patrolling especially difficult. Gavin recalls the night a fellow officer in the service company, Lt. William Ryder, got lost with a string of pack mules. (In 1941, Ryder, as a captain, would become the army's first parachute officer.)

Handling a string of pack mules at night on a

dark jungle trail is a difficult job. Bill was good
at it, but one night the mule column split and
part of it, Bill's part, became lost. By the time he
was able to phone in the company commander
was madder than hell. "Ryder," he said, "I
know you think you know where you are, but I
know I know where you are. By God, you stay
where you are until I find you. You stay lost
until I get there."⁵

In the fall of 1938, First Lieutenant Gavin returned to
the U.S. and was assigned to the 7th Infantry Division
at Vancouver, Washington, as a company commander.
The Division G-3 (plans and training) officer was Maj.
Mark Clark, later to become commander of the 5th
Army in Italy. He was trying to prepare the division for
war, but the World War I rifle, a single-shot, bolt-action
Springfield 1903, was still standard in all units. During
maneuvers a squad would pretend some two-by-fours
nailed together were a machine gun or mortar.

On 1 September 1939, Hitler's tanks and dive-bombers
swept into Poland and Europe went to war. Three days
later President Franklin Roosevelt, in one of his fireside
chats, told Americans that "this nation will remain
neutral." Yet he soon added, "I cannot ask that every
American remain neutral in thought as well."⁶ Before
the month was over, Roosevelt proclaimed a limited
"national emergency" and asked Congress to repeal the
1937 Arms Embargo Act.

In the spring of 1940, Capt. James Gavin was assigned to the Military Academy at West Point as an
instructor in the Department of Tactics. It was a fateful
spring for tacticians, as the Germans unleashed their
blitzkrieg. The Netherlands, Belgium, and France were
quickly overrun and on 14 June Paris fell. Gavin knew
that "to win we needed new ideas, we needed innova-

tion, we needed to get a quantum jump on the Germans. But how?"[7] Two of his favorite teachers, J. F. C. Fuller and Thomas "Stonewall" Jackson gave the same answer: mobility.

Fuller had long foreseen that armored warfare would restore mobility to land battles. So had several others, including the British military historian Liddell Hart, the German Gen. Heinz Guderian, the American Gen. Adna Chaffee, and a man Gavin would later come to know well, France's Gen. Charles de Gaulle. But Fuller went beyond the armor itself to the integration of communications, command, and decision needed for maximum effect.

Stonewall Jackson had had no tanks but in 1862, in the Shenandoah Valley of Virginia, he had split Union forces by striking swiftly in unexpected places. In 1940, Gavin made several visits to this battle area, reliving how Jackson's quick surprise attacks on the rear and flanks of the Armies of Virginia trapped Gen. John Pope and sent the Union forces toward Bull Run. It seemed to Gavin that our own Civil War was more like World War II than World War I.

But in 1940 the kind of mobility needed was in the air. As early as World War I the ill-fated Billy Mitchell had suggested parachute troops. The Russians had staged large-scale airborne maneuvers around Kiev in 1930. But in general airplanes were still thought of in military terms as a supplementary way of moving soldiers to an existing battleground. To link up an airborne striking force with other attack elements into a whole new type of tactical operation required a broad reorganization of communications and command structure.

By the spring of 1941, U.S. airborne forces were still only about the size of a full battalion, and some skeptics thought they should only be used for occasional raids. Gavin recalled the words of Gen. G. B. Lindsay in a book called *The War on the Civil and Military Fronts:*

Whenever a new weapon, or new tactical meth-
od, is introduced, it is always looked upon with
the gravest suspicion. That is one reason why a
study of the History of War is so important. . . .
Such a study shows that the human mind has
been slow to grasp the possibilities of the new
arrival and to adopt the tactics which will put it
to the best use. In fact, as in the case of the tank,
the new arrival has usually been treated as an
adjunct to and clothed in, the tactics of the older
arms.

In April 1941, Gavin applied for airborne duty and
parachute training. On 1 May the superintendent of the
Military Academy answered:

H.Q.U.S.M.A. West Point, NY, May 1, 1941, TO
THE ADJUTANT GENERAL, WAR DE-
PARTMENT, WASHINGTON, D.C.
  1. Disapproved.
  2. I can appreciate Captain Gavin's desire for
assignment to one of the parachute battalions.
However, in order to replace him, it would be
necessary to have an officer of equal ability
ordered to this station, and inasmuch as he has
been here less than a year, he is now approaching his maximum usefulness to the Corps of
Cadets. Further, so far as I know, he is not
peculiarly fitted for this type of duty. . . .[8]

Undefeated, Gavin decided the superintendent's real
problem was in finding a replacement for him. His old
friend Maj. Bill Kean, then in the personnel office of the
chief of infantry in Washington, helped him find a list
of officers the superintendent had wanted assigned to
The Point the previous year. The replacement was

found after several trips to the capital, and in July Gavin was ordered to parachute training at Ft. Benning, Georgia.

Meanwhile on 21 May the Germans had begun the "first all-airborne invasion in history," attacking British-defended Crete with "10,000 to 12,000" parachute troops.[9] Soon denied use of its own Cretan airfields, the Royal Air Force had to withdraw its planes. Despite hard fighting and heavy German casualties, by 29 May the capital of Canaea fell to the Germans.

The commandant of the Parachute School at Ft. Benning when Gavin began his training there was an old colleague from the Philippines, Col. William Ryder. Gavin found that jumping from an airplane was not too difficult physically, but it called for a certain psychological attitude. He realized that "the nearest thing to jumping out of an airplane is riding a reluctant horse over a difficult jump. Giving him the legs and going in with a bad spill in prospect seems to call for the same kind of mental discipline as jumping from a plane. They have in common a high degree of mixed apprehension and elation."[10]

Within a month he had completed his jump training and was given command of Company C, 503d Parachute Infantry Regiment. A few months later he was promoted to major and transferred to battalion headquarters, then to the top parachute headquarters of the army, the Provisional Parachute Group commanded by Brig. Gen. William Lee. He was made S-3, in charge of plans and training, and assigned to write the army's first manual on employment of airborne forces. During this time he spent a brief tour of duty at the army's Command and General Staff School at Ft. Leavenworth. Here, instead of innovative thinking, Gavin was dismayed to find a continuing resistance to the expansion of airborne forces and tactics. Many of the older

officers seemed to believe that significant air mobility
was at least a generation away. Then on 7 December
1941 came the Japanese attack on Pearl Harbor, which
shocked the country into action.

When Gavin returned to Ft. Bragg and the airborne
S-3 job, new equipment was becoming available. New
tactics were being rapidly developed, and a new airborne division had been authorized. With General Lee,
Gavin went to Washington to help choose the division—
the 82nd. It was activated in the fall of 1942, with Gavin
commanding one of its three regiments, the 505th Parachute Infantry. With new paratroop units and the pressures of wartime came fast promotions. Gavin had
spent ten years moving from second lieutenant to captain, from platoon leader to company commander. He
moved from captain to full colonel, commanding a regiment, in about two years.

The 82nd Division immediately went into training at
Ft. Benning with the usual high morale of units that feel
they are something special. All the officers and men
were volunteers. The men got an extra $50 a month, the
officers $100. They wore shiny, high jump boots, and
winged insignia on their tunics. All were trained in
hand-to-hand combat. But the most unusual thing
about them was that they jumped out of airplanes. As
their white chutes filled the Georgia skies, motorists
often stopped their cars to watch in amazement.

Turning an infantryman into a paratrooper took four
weeks of rigorous training. The first stage was primarily a test of physical stamina, with running, rope
climbing, obstacle courses, and calisthenics. Almost
every soldier was exposed to this, but the would-be
troopers had to exercise so hard that some men would
drop from sheer exhaustion.

The second stage was a simulated jump through a
mock airplane door mounted on a wooden platform

thirty-four feet above the ground. Strapped in the same harness he would use in a real jump but without a chute above, the trainee would leap from the platform, his harness attached to a steel cable running fifty yards from his initial jump position. Once he felt the snap of his harness, he would reach up, grab the "risers," and sail freely down the cable. Then, suspended two feet above the ground for as long as twenty minutes at a time, he would manipulate the lines. A vital step in the training, this was often painful. Groins ached from the tight harness. Blood circulation was sometimes cut off. Some called it the "nutcracker operation."

In the third stage the men went higher into the air, on a 250-foot tower. Chutes were attached to large metal rings, then raised to the top of the tower. As the trooper moved upward the chute would expand, while sergeants shouted instructions to the trainee—how to check the wind, how to pull the lines to control chute movements this way and that. If a man made a mistake and drifted into the tower it would be some time before he got to earth again, as there were no ladders.

The fourth stage was the real thing. It began with learning how to pack your own parachute, and ended with jumps from the door of a C-47 transport plane, twelve hundred feet above a drop zone. By the time a trooper got the final command to "stand up and hook up" he had already learned the physical techniques of jumping. Now the important thing was mental attitude. Certainly there were some who wondered if they would really jump or not. (According to one old joke, a veteran chutist was asked how many jumps he had made and he said, "None, but I've been pushed twenty times.") A few failed at this point. But for most, so filled by now with a "superman" feeling, not to have jumped would have been tantamount to committing suicide.

There were four daylight jumps, and one at night.

There were the inevitable broken bones and pulled muscles. But once the jumps were made the volunteer became a full-fledged parachute infantryman, complete with the winged insignia that marked him as a member of the newest and most exclusive fraternity in the armed forces.

While the individual soldier was preoccupied with learning to jump, Gavin and his fellow officers knew that their challenge went far beyond getting men out of planes and onto the ground. Assembly techniques, signals for night operations, and the problems of supply and logistical support, were studied repeatedly. They wanted to prove that what many of the older officers still thought would be a scattered and disorganized mass of troops could, in fact, become a close-knit fighting force capable of sustained combat soon after landing. Yet even then Gavin knew no one was quite sure how this new arm would be used. They would have to prove themselves on the battlefield.

Under Gavin the 505th became one of the toughest of the new parachute units. In training he drove his men hard, but the troopers knew he was a soldier up from the ranks, one of them, and that he would go to bat for them when they needed him, both on and off the post. One incident Gavin would long remember involved a roadside inn called "Cotton Fish Camp." As he recalled it,

> It seems as though a trooper had been mistreated at the Inn the evening before. The following night several squads of troopers from the 505th decided to take over the camp. They deployed some distance away in a skirmish line in good combat style and began to close in on the camp. Rumor of their intentions had preceded them, however, and as they got close to the camp, they found themselves confronted by the State Police. They were all promptly arrested.

Gavin addresses men of the 505th Parachute Infantry Regiment in
Africa, June 1943.

Above: John "Beaver" Thompson of the *Chicago Tribune* talks with Gavin a day after the Sicily jump.

Right: King George VI and the youngest general in the U.S. Army inspect the 82nd Airborne Divisional Headquarters.

Above: SACEUR reviews the 82nd Airborne at his headquarters tw
weeks before Gavin assumed divisional command. Left to right: Gavi
Eisenhower, Ridgway, Brereton.

Top right: Gavin on maneuvers with British officers in preparation f
the Normandy invasion.

Bottom right: Gavin inspects his troops during the Battle of the Bulg
December 1944.

Gavin and Ridgway confer during the Battle of the Bulge.

British award ceremony in Munchen-Gladbach, Germany, 30 March 1945. American generals in front row: McClain, Kean, Gerow, Hodges, Simpson, Collins, Gavin. Field Marshal Montgomery wears the beret.

The commandant of U.S. forces in Berlin, Major General Gavin, inspects troops with his Soviet counterpart, Field Marshal Zukov.

Gavin speaks at the victory parade in New York City. *Yale Joel.* © Time Inc. 1946.

The following morning there were 27 of them in the main Post Guard House at Fort Benning. To a young regimental commander, that was a disastrous turn of events. But I thought that I might retrieve the situation, so I called on the Provost Marshal in person and assured him that if he would let me take them out of the Guard House . . . I could handle them myself. . . . I personally marched them back to camp and that evening took the entire regiment on a long all-night march down through the cane brakes in the bottoms of the Chattahoochee River. It was a Saturday night and we maneuvered one battalion against two through the night. At daylight we were resupplied by parachute. Sunday evening, I marched them back to camp . . . I never had another incident like that."[11]

Another collision between the 505th and post officialdom is still remembered as the "Gypsy Rose Lee Case." Gavin remembered that in early 1943 he sent his public relations officer, Capt. Barney Oldfield, to a meeting at post headquarters where officers were planning Easter Sunday breakfast for the purpose of selling war bonds to the soldiers.

Evidently the meeting droned on for some time, inconclusively, when Oldfield announced that he had an idea. He said that he knew Gypsy Rose Lee, who was then appearing in *Stars and Garters* in New York, and he said that he would be happy to telephone her and ask her to come to Fort Benning after the last Saturday night performance. . . . Before she appeared on stage, they would have her take off her clothes and they would then cover her from top to bottom with war bonds, the higher priced bonds being strategically placed on her anatomy. Members of the audience would then be asked to bid on the bonds, and as they bought them, they would be removed from her body.

The idea was enthusiastically received. Everyone was excited about it and Barney Oldfield called her and she accepted the invitation. The word spread around the Post like wild fire and it was doubtful that the gymnasium would be able to hold the crowd that would certainly be there.

All went well until about a week before the affair, when the Post Commander got wind of it. "What is this," he demanded to know, "a strip tease artist attending an Easter morning breakfast in the Post gym?" He stopped it at once. . . . Not long after this I received a complaint from the Office of the Post Commander. The Regimental Adjutant of the 505th came into my office and told me that one of our troopers had been arrested for having sexual intercourse with a young lady on the lawn of the Courthouse in Phenix City. The question he was asked from Post Headquarters was "What am I going to do about it?" referring to me. "Well," I replied, "in view of the fact that the young man will be asked to give his life for his country in the next few months, I suggest we give him a medal." I heard nothing further of it.[12]

The post commander then was Col. Walter S. Fulton, a 1904 graduate of West Point, and, as Oldfield recalls, his displeasure with the antics of the 505th went beyond Gypsy Rose Lee and frolics on courthouse lawns. In an article written many years later, Oldfield said Gavin not only got a rebuke from the post commander for sending such a zany representative to the war bond meeting, he was also told that the colonel didn't want to see the "Static Line" on the newsracks in the officers club any more. It was, Fulton said, in "bad taste." The "Static Line," named for the line in the C-47s that released the paratroopers' chutes when they jumped, was the 505th's newspaper, one of the best-read service publications on the post. It had recently horrified the post with its announcement of the birth of the first battalion commander's new son who had arrived, the "Static Line" reported, in "chutese," with a "good downward pull."[13]

This order to remove the paper was only temporary. Shortly afterward, Gavin said, "We invited the Colonel and Mrs. Fulton to the Alabama training area for a regimental review. It was a day full of activities and they enjoyed it very much. It gave us an opportunity to exchange some ideas."[14] A few days later the offending newspaper was back on the post, and relations with the post commander were greatly improved.

Ft. Benning in 1943 was more than a center of infantry tactics. It was a testing ground for new infantry weapons. Gavin was constantly on the lookout for new equipment that could be carried into battle by his paratroopers. One day when he was looking at a weapons display he came across a table covered with a blanket. He asked what was under the blanket and was told that it was a new secret weapon. Finally he dragged out the information that the new weapon was a bazooka—a light, easily carried tube with a "shape-charge" shell that could punch holes in tanks. As he felt the form beneath the covering, he realized that here was something his troopers would soon be using against the armor of the German *wehrmacht*.[15]

By the summer of 1943, less than a year after he had taken command, Colonel Gavin and his three thousand troopers of the 505th were at Ft. Bragg, ready to be shipped overseas. Among the officers who saw Gavin's outfit arrive was Brig. Gen. Anthony McAuliffe of the 101st Airborne Divison, who would later become a popular hero for his stand at Bastogne. He thought the 505th "was the best regiment I had seen, and we had three very good ones, we thought, in the 101st. I was very impressed. . . ."[16]

The real test of the 505th was imminent. After maneuvers in the Sahara, the troopers would be poised for their first combat action in early July.

III. *The Crucible*

Since early afternoon on 9 July 1943, a strong *sirocco* had blown from the desert across Tunisia. Though the wind was strong enough to cancel most aerial maneuvers, more than two hundred C-47s were warming up for takeoff in the twilight. Beside the planes, weighted down with combat gear, the thirty-four hundred paratroopers of the 505th assembled around their jumpmasters. They knew they were headed for action, but for most of them the first hint of where they were going came in the written orders they were given only minutes before they boarded the planes:

Soldiers of the 505th Parachute
Combat Team

Tonight you embark upon a combat mission for which our people and the free people of the world have been waiting two years.

You will spearhead the landing of an American force upon the island of Sicily. Every preparation has been made to eliminate the element of chance. You have been given the means to do the job and you are backed by the largest assemblage of airpower in the world's history. The eyes of the world are upon you. The hopes and prayers of every American go with you.

Since it is our first fight at night, you must use the countersign and avoid firing on each other. The bayonet is the night fighter's best weapon. Conserve your water and ammunition.

The term "American Parachutist" has become synonymous with courage of a high order. Let us carry the fight to the enemy and make the American Parachutist feared and respected through all his ranks. Attack violently. Destroy him wherever found.

I know you will do your job.

Good landing, good fight, and good luck.

COLONEL GAVIN[1]

Gavin himself was among the jumpmasters, and would jump from the leading plane of his formation. For weeks he and his officers had studied the terrain, the aerial reconnaissance photos, the road networks, the German and Italian strong points. His orders from Gen. Omar Bradley, II Corps commander, called for the 505th combat team, reinforced, to drop during the night northeast of Gela near the coast of southern Sicily, to capture and secure high ground, to disrupt enemy communications, and on D day to aid the 1st U.S. Infantry Division in seizing the landing field at Ponte Olivio.

Aside from the wind, the weather looked good for the first large combat jump to be completed entirely at night. The moon was nearly full. The men would fly in nine-ship formations, with about one and one-half minutes between flights. The aerial column would take thirty-six minutes to pass a given point. If all went as planned, Gavin and his thirty-four hundred troopers and reinforcements would be on the ground in Sicily before the moon set, with several hours before daylight to set up defensive organization and operations against the enemy.

In one plane, carrying a portable typewriter instead of a rifle, was John Thompson of the *Chicago Tribune,* the only reporter to jump with the 505th in Sicily. Thompson, known to Gavin and his men as "Beaver" because of the shape of his beard, would later describe the flight in one of several stories:

> The sun was now down behind the horizon. Engines had been warmed and wheeled out to the landing strip. Promptly at 8:55 the pilot gunned our motors and we roared down the runway, lifting into the air on schedule.
>
> For another 20 minutes we circled the airport until all ships of the group had followed us up and we were flying in formation, while overhead there passed scores and scores of other formations due to land just ahead of us.
>
> It was still light as we headed out to sea, with the moon gleaming palely overhead. Just before we left some staff bookkeeper had handed the adjutant a sheaf of forms to be filled out later, but as we soared toward battle the adjutant gravely let the papers flutter out the open jump door to snow down on Arabs below.
>
> Once over the sea, our formation came down

> to wave top level. This was the safest way to
> escape detection by enemy aircraft—"flying on
> deck" as the aviators say. But it was a disquiet-
> ing sensation to skim along just above the
> water, now flecked with white caps from a stiff
> wind. . . .[2]

During the three hours and twenty minutes of the flight,
Gavin checked island landfalls against his watch. Time
and landfalls did not coordinate, and he realized that
the pilot was not on the planned course. As they came in
from the sea in the moonlight, Thompson later reported,

> the terrain looked unfamiliar. . . . But a red light
> flashed from pilot controls.
>
> The red light meant we would be over our
> objective in a few minutes. They passed quick-
> ly. The green jump light flickered, there was a
> rush down the aisle to the door, and in a mo-
> ment we were hurtling through space. . . .
>
> A brilliant glare illuminated the ground, re-
> vealing an olive grove instead of the expected
> wheat field. For a moment most of us thought
> the ground troops had set up flares and were
> opening fire. Then the sickening realization
> came that the flare was from one of our own
> transports which had broken in two and had
> burst into flames.
>
> The next moment we were landing. . . .[3]

Gavin was right to think that the terrain was un-
familiar. Instead of landing northeast of Gela, where in
a few hours Maj. Gen. Terry Allen's 1st Infantry Division would be hitting the beaches, they had landed far
to the southeast. The strong wind had pushed them
more than fifty miles from the planned drop zone.

Before dawn everyone realized the 505th had landed in the wrong area. The combat team was badly scattered, but as Gavin began a forced march—half running, half walking—toward Gela with two officers and three enlisted men, they were joined by other troopers. Gavin headed for Biazza Ridge, a spur held by a reinforced battalion of the Herman Goering Division with other German units in reserve, including tanks and artillery.

Other groups of troopers were fighting as they moved northwest. Following Gavin's orders to destroy the enemy wherever found, they struck at enemy pillboxes along the coast or further inland along the highways. With antitank weapons, grenades, and well-aimed rifle fire, they forced the Italians and a few Germans to surrender. But on the edges of Gela, Allen's 1st Division met German armored reserves and was forced to fall back.

Gavin saw that the strong German armored forces on Biazza Ridge could drive a dangerous wedge between the 1st and 45th Divisions. By ten o'clock on the morning of 11 July, he reached his target with about two hundred paratroopers and a few light artillery pieces. Thompson described the action:

> Despite the smallness of his force, the colonel went into position on the lower hill in the orchard and then began working through the tall grass, gnarled little trees and vineyards.
>
> The armored grenadiers—for that is what the opposition proved to be—fought back with their fast firing machine guns, mausers, artillery, and mortars.
>
> Our first rush shoved the enemy back up and over the hill altogether. He outnumbered us then about three to one. The troopers had him

on the run, but he came back strong with more artillery fire and then tanks, not only Mark IV's but his huge Mark VI Tiger tanks mounting 88-millimeter guns in the turret.

The next hour was our worst. Everyone expected an attack by the tanks in force and it looked as if there were a good chance that we would be overrun. . . . Then the colonel called on his last hope and ordered three available howitzers wheeled up for direct fire. I saw one gun come up this hill into position. One trooper rode its barrel while others muscled the piece up the slope to a ridge beside a small white stone house. The tanks began registering hits all around the gun almost immediately, but, with the coolness of veterans, these men placed their gun. They opened fire at 800 yards, knocking out two tanks. . . . At 8:10, our tanks opened and we charged in two waves while the Germans replied with intense mortar fire and sweeping machine gun fire. Overhead their Messerschmitts prowled to observe or strafe.

Half an hour later it was quiet. And in the gloom of the gathering night our men came back to their lines while the tanks withdrew, having destroyed from the rear a huge Tiger tank.

We counted many dead and wounded, but it was a victory beyond question. The attack had driven the enemy off his hill back through the village and he had abandoned tons of equipment. In fact, a reconnaissance later showed he retreated completely from this sector.[4]

Gavin's troopers, in their first combat action, had proved the value of their arduous training. Despite their dispersal on landing, they had captured strong points in the path of the main invasion forces.

Paratroopers had come into their own. Later Gavin would write that "Sicily, in July of 1943, was the birthplace of American Airborne technique. . . . The toddling tot that later became the First Allied Airborne Army was born in Sicily and survived a very rugged delivery."[5] Gavin himself won the first of his two Distinguished Service Crosses in this action, and many of his men were also decorated for gallantry. His citation was signed "by command of Lieutenant General Patton," commander of the 7th Army who had taken charge at Gela. Shortly after the Biazza Ridge action Gavin met with Patton in his command post, which he described later in a letter to his daughter Barbara:

> I have always liked [Patton] since . . . Sicily when I came into his CP after a very trying two days and three nights. He took a big flask out of his hip pocket and gave me a drink. The situation seemed to call for more than just "thank you" and I made a speech about being honored to drink from the flask of such a fine soldier. Not to be outdone, he came right back with a much better one. I later came to know him rather well and learned to regard his combat effectiveness with great respect. Now, in retrospect, the speeches seem melodramatic and perhaps out of place, but at the time they were quite proper and in order. People seem to get stirred up emotionally in combat and sometimes do things that at a later time seem odd.[6]

Altogether, the Allies had put more than a hundred and sixty thousand men into Sicily, including three U.S. infantry divisions of Patton's 7th Army and the

British, Canadian, and French forces of Montgomery's British 8th Army. Within a few days, these units were linked and the whole southeastern end of Sicily from Licatta to the edge of the Catanian plain was under Allied control. But there had been twelve Italian and four German divisions, about two hundred and fifty thousand men, on the island. A few days after the initial drop of the 505th, the 82nd Airborne Division under Maj. Gen. Matthew Ridgway was assembled and fought its way across Sicily in five days and five nights, capturing more than twenty-three thousand prisoners.

As the fighting subsided, new social relationships sprang up between the troops and the civilian population, and commanders faced the inevitable problem of veneral disease. In Hawaii and Arizona, for instance, military police and officers would be stationed in red-light districts to keep order among the soldiers and prostitutes. Overseas, some commanders tried to ignore the problem. But when soldiers were kept from women, the unit's fighting effectiveness and morale suffered.

Gavin met the challenge by opening a brothel for his troops. Much later, Thompson of the *Chicago Tribune* recalled the operation in detail:

> Very few people actually know this episode in the General's life. Indeed, the only proof hangs on the wall of my home . . . an order—instructing the commanding officer of the 505th to open and operate a brothel for the use of his troops. It details, paragraph by paragraph, just how the operation is to be conducted, even going so far as to set the fee to be charged every trooper for the services of a young lady. . . . This order in my house is the original. Nor was it signed. After all, it would never do for Major General Matthew B. Ridgway, 82nd Division Com-

mander, to place his name on an order of this kind—particularly since the Army officially never recognized the legality of any brothel. The order came into my possession from Gavin. ... When I found Gavin [in Sicily] the first thing he said was, "You must see my house." Naturally, I assumed he had taken over a Sicilian chateau for his billet. The place, as we approached by jeep was imposing enough. It had been the two-story home of a wealthy land owner, surrounded by a high circular wall for protection. . . . Off to one side of the first floor, the doc had set up a pro-station through which every GI had to pass after leaving the gals. . . . Gavin, incidentally, was never apologetic about his "house." Rather, he was proud of it, for a simple and basic reason. The 505th never had a single case of rape in its area—a rare phenomenon, for the same could not be said of any other unit, at least in Sicily.[7]

In addition to specifying hours and fees, the order Thompson cites authorized a medical detachment to:

a. examine all men entering the premises and refuse entrance to anyone with suspicion of venereal disease. Such individuals will be reported to the Unit Surgeon.
b. insure that all troops who enter the building receive the necessary prophylaxis prior to departure.
c. insure proper sanitation of the house and its inmates.[8]

By 20 August, the 82nd was back in Tunisia. Near the city of Kairouan, they began training for the upcoming invasion of the Italian mainland at Salerno. But Gavin knew they might have another target, the city of Rome itself.

As early as July 1943, while the 82nd was still fighting in Sicily, it was apparent that the Italian Fascist regime was approaching collapse. With many soldiers captured in Africa and others scattered on fronts from southern Europe to Russia, the army could not defend the Italian mainland. Some soldiers seemed willing to join the partisan guerrillas against the Germans if the chance arose. On 24 July Mussolini was replaced by the staid Marshal Pietro Badoglio, Italy's most prestigious old soldier. The new regime placed Italy under martial law, put Mussolini under arrest, renounced his German friends, and rallied behind King Victor Emmanuel. Mussolini himself was soon rescued by German paratroopers, but this did little to restore Italy's will to continue the war.

At this juncture Italian army commander General Castellano suggested that the Allies drop parachute troops on Rome, capture it with the aid of Italian troops in the area, and thus avoid a long costly struggle up the boot of Italy against German defenders. The Italians would surrender unconditionally, support the Allied operations, and announce an armistice.

The plan, called Giant Two, was to drop the entire 82nd Airborne Division around and on Rome on the nights of 8 and 9 September. The operation would begin at 6:30 P.M. on 8 September, when General Eisenhower would announce the Italian armistice through Radio Algiers. At the sound of Eisenhower's voice, the 82nd's 504th Regiment would leave Sicily for airfields at Cerveteri, northwest of Rome. Gavin's 505th would follow the next night, jumping on airfields at Littoria, Glidonia, and Cnetocelle—even closer to the center of Rome. The rest of the division, plus the 325th Glider Regiment, would land inside the city. Artillery support would follow after an amphibious landing on the night of 9 September. In preparation for this mission, the 82nd was flown from Africa to Sicily on 4 and 5 September.

Meanwhile, General Eisenhower, aware of the high risk involved, sent Gen. Maxwell Taylor, assistant division commander of the 82nd, and Col. William T. Gardner on a secret personal reconnaissance of Rome. When he arrived at Marshall Badoglio's villa, General Taylor was astounded to hear that the Italians wanted to call off the drop because of the sudden arrival of new German troop units in the area. They also wanted to postpone the armistice to a time more advantageous to them.

Taylor had been equipped with the code word "innocuous" to be used if needed for cancellation of the operation. But he first sent a message saying Giant Two seemed "impossible." Eisenhower received this message at about 8:00 A.M. on 8 September—less than eleven hours before he was to announce the armistice that would touch off the air drop on the Italian capital. And by this time the 82nd's troopers in Sicily were already being issued ammunition for the operation.

Angered by the Italian hesitation, Eisenhower made it clear to Badoglio that he intended to announce the armistice anyway. Badoglio then changed his position again and read the armistice notice to his own people in accordance with the original plan. By this time, however, General Taylor suspected the Italians might not follow through on the Rome operation. At 11:35 A.M. on 8 September, he sent Eisenhower the coded message "Situation Innocuous," which canceled Giant Two.

At 3:30 A.M. on 9 September, Gen. Mark Clark's 5th Army landed at Salerno. An unexpectedly strong German force drove a two-mile wedge into the American beachhead. Within hours, 120 troop-carrying aircraft dropped Gavin and nineteen hundred men of his 505th behind the beachhead.

In a letter to his daughter on 21 September Gavin said of the Salerno jump, "I sweated this one out a bit, as the boys say, but it turned out to be the easiest jump for some time." However, another of the 82nd's regiments, the 504th, met disaster. Through an error in identification several of its planes were shot down by U.S. Navy antiaircraft guns. At the time of Gavin's letter security prevented any mention of this, or even of the name Salerno. He said only that he was "somewhere in Italy."[9]

Both Sicily and Salerno were learning experiences as well as victories to Gavin. After Sicily he had decided that the troopers would no longer blacken their faces for night operations. It was more important for them to be visible to one another than invisible to the enemy. And they would no longer use "crickets" (small metal snappers) as signals. They would rely instead on the more reliable oral challenge and response. Plane loads of men and weapons would be better balanced, so that if one were dropped in the wrong area the unit would still be fully equipped. Every assembly technique improvised during the first hours in Sicily was studied and restudied for possible future use. German tanks had been a major obstacle, so bazookas and mines would be distributed throughout the flight.[10]

While the colonel at thirty-six was absorbing new tactical ideas, he was also thinking about broader issues. His mental growth was revealed in his letters to his daughter Barbara, then living with her mother in Washington, D.C. Mixed in with material that any father would write to a youngster in her twelfth through fourteenth years—questions about school and summer camp, warnings to be careful while swimming and on hikes—and descriptions of his own encounters with

African heat, with Sicilian fleas and mosquitoes, are such paragraphs as:

> I have frequently written you of the quality of native Arabs. . . . As a racial group they are like no other people in the world; perhaps it is their religion that sets them apart.
>
> The evaluation of a people is made, in the last analysis, in two ways: by the world at large, and by the people themselves. To the world at large, the measure of worth of a racial group is evaluated in terms of their creative contributions to the arts, sciences, and welfare of the human race as a whole. To the people, the race is measured by their own happiness and contentment. . . . I will always remember that the Mexicans were extremely contented with their lot, whereas we were sorry for them. . . . The Arabs are a totally satisfied racial group who want nothing from us other than to be left alone.[11]

In another letter from North Africa, the man who would later be called a "spoiled general" commented on the Detroit race riots and the defiance of government authority by United Mine Workers' President John L. Lewis:

> It makes me feel uneasy. Everyone knows that one of the things we are fighting for is the right of everyone to do and say as he pleases, as long as it is not contrary to public interest. But that stuff doesn't seem right. To the soldier mind, a respect for constituted authority must be a cornerstone of our social structure if it is to continue to exist. . . . When this war ends, I think I

would like to be a curate in an out-of-the-way pastorate with nothing to do but care for the flowers and meditate on the wickedness of the world. I have had more than enough excitement and danger to do for a lifetime.[12]

He was concerned about the local civilian population:

We all read of conditions of these axis controlled countries, but none of us really appreciated how deplorable things were until we encountered conditions here. The state and local fascists took everything. Most of every crop and just about all the meat goes to the individuals in the inside of the local political circle. There appeared to be no way for the people to beat the system. They are about all pinch-faced and hungry. We have had only a form of hard tack since our arrival and several days ago a nearby town baker agreed to sell us some bread. When we went to get it, it turned out to be flour that he kept solely for the Italian Army and politicans; at that very moment there were crowds of hungry civilians outside asking for bread. We ordered the baker to give it to them, much to his dismay.[13]

From somewhere just above Naples, Gavin wrote:

After a very active two weeks, the 505th had the privilege of capturing Naples. It is a lovely place, although at the moment rather badly off. The Germans destroyed all water and lights, opened the prisons, destroyed all docks, food stores, and so forth. On a city of 700,000 that is pretty hard.

I have just been transferred from 505th to Division Headquarters, where I have the job of Assistant Division Commander. I do not particularly mind, since it entitles me to a very nice room in an excellent hotel. For the first time since May 10, I slept in a bed last night. Really didn't sleep well—it was too soft.[14]

Thereafter his letters were less concerned with his actual duties as he had become involved in the top secret planning of airborne operations for the Normandy invasion. It was apparent, however, that he missed his troops and old way of living. In a letter of 21 October 1943 he wrote:

You all seem to keep guessing my whereabouts and, of course, I am in no position to tell you, despite the revelations of the current press. Incidentally, reading the latest *Time* I have received, September 27th, I believe, the Fifth Army had a very hard time in the Salerno Bay area—very, very interesting. It is, if I may say so, very gratifying to at least read news accounts from the States that have us met with something besides flowers and platitudes. I believe that I speak for many when I say it is at times disheartening to read of how the peace is to be settled and of how certain American arms will triumph with ease when we in our own hearts know of the hunger, heartaches, and graves yet ahead of us.[15]

He already knew that many of those graves would be in Normandy. By the end of 1943, he was in England helping plan the biggest airborne operation in history.

Two full U.S. airborne divisions, the 82nd and the

101st, along with British airborne forces, would make the initial drop. In addition to parachutes, hundreds of gliders towed by transport planes would be used to land men and combat equipment. By early 1944, aerial photos showed that the Germans were building large numbers of antiairborne obstacles on the Cherbourg peninsula, in expectation of just such a landing. The 82nd was originally scheduled to land on "Hill 110" near St. Sauveur le Vicomte, about eighteen miles south of Cherbourg. Reconnaissance photos showed the area was full of "Rommel's asparagus," poles six to twelve inches in diameter and eight to twelve feet long, driven into the ground about seventy-five feet apart. Later Gavin would find that many of the poles were booby-trapped with artillery shells and land mines. Fortunately, shortly before the invasion, the drop zones for the 82nd were moved about ten miles east of this area.

As D day neared, Gavin later wrote,

> we memorized the terrain, the drop areas, and the road nets, and we memorized all plans and orders so that no man would have to take a marked paper into combat.... And we held war games on scaled sand tables... until every man knew not only his own mission but that of his probable neighbors in combat. . . .[16]

In the darkness before dawn of 6 June, General Eisenhower pressed a button that flashed the "go" signal to airdromes and ports around and across England. Airborne divisions ran across fields to the transports and gliders. Much of the amphibious invasion fleet was still waiting to sail when the first airborne troopers leaped from the open doors of the transports over France, on top of a tough enemy. They had to fight literally from the moment they hit the ground. Under the command of Col. William Ekman, the 505th regiment landed near St. Mère Église on the Cherbourg Peninsula, at the western end of the sixty-mile Allied invasion front. St. Mère Église was the first town captured.

During thirty-three days of combat in Normandy without relief or replacements, the 82nd fought five enemy divisions and immobilized the 265th and 91st German Infantry Divisions. One outstanding example of the fighting spirit of the 82nd was Lt. Col. Benjamin Vandervort, commander of the 2nd Battalion of the 505th Parachute Infantry Regiment, who broke an ankle in the jump but refused to be evacuated. Gavin himself won the second of his Distinguished Service Crosses in the Normandy action.

As soon as he could, Gavin wrote a short note home to daughter "Butch," to quash reports that he had been wounded:

> Let's get something straight. I haven't been wounded. You embarrass me. There have been so many wounded who deserve sympathy and consideration. But not Pappy. I just had my face scratched, just that and nothing more, really. A day or two later I was talking with someone about it and I couldn't find the scratches.[17]

In August 1944 Major General Ridgway, who had commanded the 82nd since 1942, was made a corps commander and the division was turned over to "Gentleman Jim Gavin." His family background and the fact that he had risen from the ranks were common knowledge in the division. The men were proud that Gavin was the youngest division commander since the Civil War. They liked the way he laughed quickly, and how he punctuated his stories with, "This is true." They enjoyed the way he called them "troopers" and very often, despite his own youth, referred to them as "son." They liked his equanimity, and the way he made them feel at ease when he talked with them. They appreciated that he put questions to them, not just orders, and how he inspected their food and sleeping quarters.

Their new commander was convinced that they and "all airborne soldiers . . . have a rendezvous with greatness." He wrote: "I have a thousand ideas and I'm going to carry them through in combat and out, with zeal and determination, come what may."[18]

By mid-September, a little more than three months after the Normandy invasion, Belgium and Luxembourg had been liberated and the Allies were making their first thrusts across the German border. The Netherlands, however, remained almost entirely in German hands. British, Canadian, and Polish troops were meeting stiff resistance as they attempted to cross the Belgian border into Holland. Again Eisenhower called on the airborne forces. On the night of 16–17 September the largest airborne force ever assembled—the First Allied Airborne Army—began its strike behind enemy lines in Holland by parachute and glider. Simultaneously, infantry and armored units launched strong ground attacks intended to drive a corridor through to the airborne troops.

The ultimate objective of the 82nd was to seize and hold the Grave and Nijmegen Bridges and the high ground to the south of Nijmegen, as well as several other bridges over a canal east of Grave. The long Nijmegen Bridge was a vital part of the main traffic arteries of Holland. The German strong points commanding the approaches to the railroad bridge and the highway bridge were well equipped, well entrenched, and had air support. A direct assault on the bridge was bound to fail.

General Gavin ordered the 504th Parachute Infantry Regiment to cross the Waal River to the west of the bridge, using collapsible boats. The crossing took place on the afternoon of a clear, bright day, and as the Irish Guards Armored Division of the British Second Army provided the 504th with boats, they commented that the Americans must be trying to commit suicide. But the 504th crossed the river and attacked the German positions successfully. The Irish Guards tanks covered the operation.

The 82nd completed its mission in Holland, taking the bridges after three full days of combat action. By this time the division had been in more campaigns and combat than any of the other five American airborne divisions. It had jumped in Sicily, Salerno, Normandy, and Holland. This last campaign cost approximately three thousand wounded, and eight hundred dead. As Gavin discovered when he supervised the distribution of ballots, many of the men were extremely young. At the time of the invasion of Holland, the average age in the division was twenty-two.

On the thirtieth anniversary of the Battle of the Bridges, Gavin visited the site with Cornelius Ryan, who had just completed his book on the Holland operation, *A Bridge Too Far.*

After the operation Gavin and the 82nd were stationed in the drab French village of Sissonne to rest, reequip, and get replacements. But the weeks of rest ended suddenly when German Gen. Karl Von Rundstedt launched a massive counteroffensive against American forces in the Ardennes, touching off the Battle of the Bulge. About twelve hours after Gavin received the alert on 14 December, his twelve thousand men headed through Bastogne to the St. Vith area. Gavin's mission was to establish a corridor and free the remnants of four American divisions trapped in the St. Vith pocket.

"Hell, it's normal for paratroopers to be surrounded on all sides," remarked Jack Norton, division G-3, when he reviewed the mission.[19] But some who fought in the campaign said that fighting the enemy was not as bad as fighting the winter. A man wounded badly had to be taken to shelter at once, or he would die from exposure to the cold. Some soldiers waded up to their waists in freezing water to blow up a bridge, working to destroy the trusses while German vehicles moved over their heads. Troopers of the 504th attacked a unit of the 1st SS Panzer Division near Cheneux, jumping on the vehicles and virtually clubbing the German tank crews to death with their rifle butts. Some of these Germans were from the group that had massacred American soldiers at Malmedy.

Gavin's old regiment, the 505th, fought for three days and nights without overcoats and blankets, and only cold C rations for food. Unable to light fires at night, they huddled together for warmth, but if they kept still some of them would freeze.

It was also during this action that another U.S. Airborne Division, the 101st, won justified fame for its heroic stand at Bastogne. Gavin himself, as acting commander of the XVIII Airborne Corps, had given the order to Brig. Gen. Anthony C. McAuliffe, acting commanding general of the 101st, to move into the Bastogne sector. Maj. Gen. Maxwell D. Taylor, the division commander, was in Washington at this time. When he heard of the German attack, he rushed back to Germany to assume command of his division.

En route to Bastogne by jeep and still dressed in "pinks and greens," then semiformal dress, he was forced to stop and take cover from German artillery fire. He halted in a place where Charles Collingwood, Walter Cronkite, and a few other war correspondents were taking shelter from the same shelling. "Taylor was so impatient at this delay," Collingwood recalled, "that after a few minutes he called his driver and both took off for Bastogne."[20]

Even before Taylor arrived, McAuliffe had rejected a German surrender ultimatum. He would soon become a popular hero for reportedly saying "nuts" to the German demand, despite his later denial that he used that word.

Finally relieved, the 82nd returned to Sissone. Throughout the fall and winter, Gavin continued his letters to Barbara whenever he could. From Holland he wrote:

> This is quite a place. The Dutch are very nice people and have very clean tidy homes. They are sincere and courageous in their desire for freedom from the Germans. They have, without exception, been very kind to us; the closer to the border they are the more intensely anti-German they are.
>
> The Germans in their homeland are rather quiet and perhaps a bit sullen. It is odd to sense the feeling of hostility after the enthusiasm of Sicily, Italy and Normandy.
>
> I am not looking forward to the Winter war we have ahead of us. Even now it is uncomfortably cold most of the time. I wear everything that I can get on but I feel as though I will never be warm again. . . . The drop was rather exciting, a bit of flak and stuff. I drew my knees up under my chin. I was very lucky, I guess. Made a fine landing, flat on my back. I was carrying so much stuff I had a hard time staggering to my feet. Every time I take something additional that I am sure I am going to need.[21]

By this time Gavin had made many friends in the press corps. The commander of a colorful outfit that made good copy for the reporters, Gavin was as open and honest with them as security would allow. He wrote his daughter that he had "talked to a lot of newspaper people lately. . . . If they are permitted to publish half of the stuff I tell them there should be some tall tales in the American press." He told her he tried, for the sake of the division,

> to have a good press and I have, as a matter of fact, some very good friends among the press. It is a fine thing for the troops to receive from home press clippings extolling their accomplishments; they feel then that the folks back home are being made aware and are appreciative of all that they are doing. It all adds up. The division gets a character and personality of its own.
>
> But in order to do this in a practical sense, it is necessary for the press to exploit the old man, the CG, if and how it can. I do not know what you read about the Division in the home papers, but it is obviously smart business to be as courteous to the press and as considerate of their requirements as we can be, and we try. Some of the finest people that I have met in the war so far have been newspaper men. Our American foreign war correspondents are almost without exception brilliant men and usually all around pretty good Joes.[22]

Through the early months of 1945, with the war nearing an end, Gavin's letters began to show an increasing concern with the postwar world. Responding to the news of President Roosevelt's death he wrote:

We will miss his leadership in world affairs in the next three or four years. I believe that every veteran who has seen war at close quarters, and death, and devastation that follows in its wake, sincerely hopes that our people will take the leadership in world affairs and insist on the establishment of peace—by the use of force if necessary. . . . We cannot depend upon the existence of peace by just getting along well together, any more than a community can depend on people just getting along well together. There will always be gangster nations, as there always are people who take advantage of others at every opportunity.[23]

The 82nd's return to Sissone was for more than a well-earned rest. Soon a tough new training program for replacements was underway, along with a new jump school operation. Few of the troopers or officers knew they were being groomed for a dramatic climax to the war in Europe, the airborne capture of Berlin.

The plan to drop on the German capital, called Operation Eclipse, had been instituted as early as November 1944 when Gen. Lewis Brereton, commander of the First Allied Airborne Army, received orders to prepare for such an action. As the plan developed, Gavin's 82nd was to land two regiments just south of Berlin's Templehoff Airdrome and block any German moves toward the field. A third regiment was to seize the airfield itself. Gavin knew it would be a tough fight. The buildings around Templehoff were like miniature fortresses. In addition, there would be difficult logistical problems of landing and receiving airborne supplies in such a concentrated combat area.

On 2 March the Allies reached the Rhine, near Dusseldorf. And five days later General Eisenhower was entertaining several senior officers at his quarters in Reims when he received word that a bridge across the Rhine had been captured by American troops at Remagen. The end of the war was clearly in sight. The 82nd's Berlin drop was canceled and Gavin's troopers joined in the rush across Germany, moving to an area north of the Elbe River to join the British for the last fighting of the war.

The German collapse was swift. On one day an entire German army of a hundred and forty-four thousand soldiers surrendered to the 82nd. On another day, some one hundred thousand enemy troops did the same. By 14 April the U.S. 9th Army had reached the Elbe and was prepared to move quickly to Berlin. Eisenhower ordered them to stop there and two days later the Russian armies launched their massive assault on Berlin from the east, entering the city on 24 April. Thus rather than drop on the German capital, or fight for it in the streets, the 82nd marched into Berlin as occupation troops. Gavin was the first American military commander in the city.

During the days in Berlin, Gavin reflected on the Americans' relationships with the French, British, and Russians, and tried to imagine what postwar Europe would be like. Although his personal and professional relationships with his counterparts were cordial, it was clear to him that difficulties lay ahead and that it would take patience and strength to deal with the Russians. He hoped for understanding, and that the United States would not slough off its hard-won victory by giving up too much too soon.

Gavin did everything he could to make sure the 82nd would not be "pushed around" in Berlin. He insisted that the troopers be sharply dressed, as well as combat-ready, at all times. One evening he impressed the Russian generals in a way they would never forget. As a mixed group recalled the wartime exploits of their troops, one Soviet officer boasted of the fierce loyalty of his men. "They will do anything I say—anything!" "So," said Gavin, "will mine." Then, turning to one of his regimental commanders, Col. Charles Billingslea, he gave a sharp and totally unexpected order: "Billingslea, jump out the window!" Billingslea immediately rose, walked to the open window, and leaped out—fracturing an ankle as he hit the street two and one-half floors below.[24]

Gavin continued to write home about the press. There were references to the publicity of the 101st Airborne Division, commanded by an officer with whom Gavin would later have deep disagreements, Maj. Gen. Maxwell Taylor. The 101st had received well-earned publicity for its heroic stand at Bastogne in the Battle of the Bulge, but apparently some of Gavin's family felt that this single action was eclipsing the fame of the 82nd, whose overall combat record was more impressive. He wrote to Barbara:

> Public relations are fascinating and in this war have been extremely interesting. There have been brilliant examples of selling the public a view for a purpose, notably Arnhem and Bastogne. They were splendidly handled from a public relations viewpoint.
>
> Never feel any animosity towards the 101st, they are grand people. As a matter of fact, I was in Bastogne with them their first night and gave them their order to stay while I joined my own crowd farther north. . . . In a public relations viewpoint, each division has a character of its own. . . . We have carefully cultivated a long range plan of making ours a steady, courageous, dependable unit that can and does do

the impossible in combat as a matter of course.
By now the press in general knows us for this;
we have a very good press. . . . The easiest thing
in this business is to get personally publicized
and this must be avoided . . . do not judge our
accomplishments too much by the newspaper
lineage; the author of the article and the quality
and publisher mean more than anything, almost more, really, than what actually happened.[25]

Despite Gavin's praise for the 101st Airborne, there
were reports of a growing rivalry between him and
Taylor which soon became more than a personal matter. Both foresaw that in the coming demobilization
there would be room for only one airborne division, and
they knew that division would be either the 82nd or the
101st. By late autumn of 1945, after the Japanese surrender, this rivalry had taken on a new symbolic signifi-
cance. The War Department's choice for the unit to lead
the victory parade on New York's Fifth Avenue had
been narrowed down to the 82nd or the 101st.

In sheer statistics, the 82nd was well ahead. It had
pioneered American airborne combat with the jump in
Sicily. It had made four combat jumps while the 101st
had made two. The 82nd had received 2 Congressional
Medals of Honor, 69 Distinguished Service Crosses, a
Distinguished Service Medal, 894 Silver Stars, 32
Legion of Merits, and 2,478 Bronze Stars. There were
also approximately 13,000 Purple Hearts. Of these decorations, Gavin himself had been awarded two Distinguished Service Crosses and the one medal, a Silver
Star, a Legion of Merit, and a Purple Heart.

Foreign decorations also abounded. The Dutch had
honored Gavin as a Grand Officer of the Order of the
Orange-Nassau, an award never before conferred on a

foreigner and normally awarded only to persons of royal blood. For gallantry in action the entire division had been awarded the Orange Lanyard of the Netherlands Wilhelms Orde, comparable to the Victoria Cross or the Congressional Medal of Honor. The Belgian Fourragere was also among the division honors, as was a French citation for gallantry in Normandy. Forty-two individuals had received British decorations. There were 53 French decorations, 14 Russian, and 73 other Dutch awards.

General Eisenhower favored the 82nd to lead the big parade and to remain on active duty, but the War Department preferred the 101st. Even before the parade issue arose, Gavin heard reports that his division was to be demobilized. On 19 September he wrote his daughter that the 82nd was to leave for home in late October. But by early October his friendship with reporters was having an effect.

> We have some wonderful friends in the press in the ETO and they are getting all excited about [the plan to demobilize the division]. They have formed what they call a crusade and at their own expense they have wired their papers and their press friends in the States protesting our demobilization. You will hear more about this. I am trying to stay out of it as much as I can. But we do have some fine friends; the Division is exceptionally well-liked by every newspaper man in the business over here and they insist that they will not sit around and see the War Department end the 82nd Airborne when other divisions are permitted to remain in the post war Army.[26]

With the 82nd's future still highly uncertain, Gavin wrote Barbara from Berlin:

We continue to prepare to leave for the U.S., still hoping that some way, somehow, the War Department will reconsider our demobilization. For one who has not been through what we have together, it is difficult to explain how we feel about this thing that the 82nd has. Elusive, indefinable, and abstract as it is, it is none the less a powerful and great thing to us. And we of course feel that it is a great thing for the American people to preserve.[27]

He enclosed a letter he had received from a lieutenant in his command, which said:

The impact of your will has, through some process of osmosis, penetrated all the layers of the Division hierarchy down to the newest private, and I think I understand now how commanders like Marlborough and Sheridan and Lawrence were able to seize the imagination of men and suspend them from it as if from a cord.[28]

By the time the 82nd came home in late 1945, as "Beaver" Thompson would recall later, "The Army saw the light."

It was announced that the 82d Division would be retained as the Army's only active duty airborne division. And so it was that the 82d, not the 101st, led the Victory Parade down 5th Avenue when the 82d was finally brought home from Germany. Gavin and the 82d were always sure that my stories had turned the tide and kept the 82d on top of the heap. They insisted on presenting me with a lovely engraved Swiss watch commemorating the event.[29]

Gavin returned by plane from Paris just in time to spend Christmas with his wife and daughter, who had lived in an attractive small apartment at 2022 Columbia Road in Washington, D.C., while Gavin was in Europe. One of the highlights of his return was his presentation to Barbara of a watch sent her by Russians who had worked with Gavin in Germany.[30]

Surely another highlight was on 12 January 1946, when Gavin led the 12,280 paratroopers of the 82nd up Fifth Avenue at the head of the biggest victory parade in U.S. history, as elements of the 101st marched behind. Between two and four million cheering people watched the parade.

Marching in the 82nd's ranks were nearly 350 black paratroopers, members of the 555th Parachute Infantry battalion, the "Triple Nickels," the nation's only all-black paratroop unit. The 555th had only recently been attached to the division for training and maneuvers at Fort Bragg, North Carolina, but Gavin had ordered that they march with him, all wearing the Orange Lanyard of the Netherlands and the red and green Belgian Fourragere. Their appearance was a symbol of Gavin's determination to proceed with racial integration in the service. In the months ahead, black officers and men would occupy positions in many echelons of the division.

After the parade, Gavin was interviewed by a reporter from the *New York Times*. He waxed enthusiastic about the opening of a "whole new era" of military tactics, then quickly added: "But I don't want any more war. Not for me, for this country or any other country."[31]

IV. *The New Era*

Few of the cheering spectators of the victory parade on Fifth Avenue worried then about the ominous new era that had opened only five months earlier when a B-29 bomber named *Enola Gay* had dropped the first atomic weapon in the history of warfare on the Japanese city of Hiroshima. In one blinding flash the bomb killed more than a hundred thousand Japanese.

The Hiroshima bombing had taken place while Gavin was still on occupation duty in Berlin. Like many other military leaders, he saw almost immediately that this "had changed the art of war for all time."[1] The atomic bomb was not the only new weapon. As early as June 1944, the Germans had fired a "robot bomb" against England. This aerodynamic missile was followed by the world's first long-range guided missile.

To some older military minds the robot bombs were not much more than interesting novelties. To others, including Gavin, they meant a whole new era of tactics and—ultimately—the decline of the manned bomber. "I could see then," Gavin later recalled, "that the parachute as a means for a man to exit from an airplane and land on the ground was rapidly becoming obsolete."[2] And he knew that huge amphibious operations like the Normandy invasion would be suicidal against an enemy equipped with missiles and nuclear warheads. These new weapons meant the end for both mass airborne and mass infantry operations.

As he took his 82nd Airborne Division to Fort Bragg early in 1946, Gavin was convinced of at least three things: atomic warheads would become more powerful and more numerous; missile systems to deliver them would become faster and farther-ranging, and—most important for him at the time—a new airborne army with radically new vehicles and tactics would have to be developed. Mobility and surprise would be the key elements, along with dispersion.

At Fort Bragg in 1946 and 1947, Gavin had the all-black 555th Parachute Infantry Battalion work out some of these innovations. The unit practiced the patterns of dispersing at a marshalling area and at an airfield while preparing for an airborne operation, under simulated atomic warfare.

This was a radical departure from the airborne marshalling activities of just a few years before. There were also changes in parachute drop patterns and assembly techniques. Simultaneously, Gavin urged the replacement of the old, reliable C-47 transport plane by an aircraft of considerably greater range, cargo load, and global performance capabilities, the C-119. Privately, and somewhat sentimentally, he would mourn the passing of the sturdy twin-engine C-47 which had carried him and his troopers on so many missions: "God, that was a wonderful airplane. I have nothing but respect for the men who built it."[3]

Remembering the plywood gliders that became "burning coffins" at the crossing of the Rhine at Wessels, he supported their replacement with gliders of tubular construction. He promoted the use of planes with small engines for short takeoff or landing capability, which evolved into the assault aircraft used for logistical and tactical support of ground operations like those in Korea and Vietnam.

The 82nd experimented in 1946 with a limited number of two-seater Bell helicopters for aerial observation, artillery spotting, liaison, command and communication, and evacuation. Now standard practice, these concepts of air mobility were then far ahead of military establishment thinking, despite the lessons of World War II. As Gavin said later:

> We had used air mobility to fly a division back and forth from Africa to Sicily, and then to commit it to Salerno to tip the scale of battle in our favor. We had used air mobility to fly a division from England to the continent at the time of the Battle of the Bulge. We had used air mobility to resupply Bastogne and to supply General Patton's fast moving Third Army. In fact, I have no doubt whatsoever that with half again as much air mobility we could have won the war in 1944 and occupied Berlin first.[4]

Obviously, a few maneuvers at Fort Bragg would not in themselves create a new airborne army. Gavin also embarked on a literary career that was to continue for nearly three decades, often to the despair of the Pentagon. He began by writing articles for service publications such as the *Infantry Journal,* recounting the lessons learned from Sicily and Normandy. As early as 1947, he wrote a piece called "The Future of Armor," published in *Combat Forces Journal* and *The Armored Cavalry Journal,* urging the development of new, light armored vehicles and new aircraft to fly them into battle. In 1948, he published his first full-length book, *Airborne Warfare.* He intended the book to be "a text that would enable students and faculty members of our [service] schools to understand how we made airborne operations work—their complexities, the organizational problems, the relationships between drop zones and target areas, supply. . . ."[5] Actually the book went far beyond the military technicalities of past airborne operations. It was, in fact, an open criticism of the military establishment's increasing reliance on improved versions of manned bombers.

Gavin assumed that though the bomb would drastically change the equipment and tactics of ground forces, such forces would still be needed to finish the work of initial air attacks.[6] "Never in the history of mankind, certainly, has anything affected man's thinking and his probably military behavior so drastically as the atomic bomb. It changes—must greatly change—our whole military thinking, organization, and tactics."[7]

He argued that the future of American ground forces, including armor, was in the air, since "only through flight can we wage a future war in accordance with the principles of surprise, mass and economy of means."[8] He also felt that the existence of airborne troops, "capable of moving anywhere on the globe on short notice, available to an international security body such as the United Nations, is our best guarantee of lasting peace."[9] He believed that if a war did occur, the new weapons meant it would have to be limited. There could be no more total victory. War no longer meant backing an enemy into a corner where he had no choice but subjugation or annihilation.

Gavin found obsolete and simplistic the idea that war and peace are distinct and separate phases of a nation's life. He believed that "most thoughtful people recognize ... there is economic war, cold war, espionage, guerrilla war, limited war, the war of ideas, etc. A nation faces challenges to its power and exerts its influence on others in a variety of shifting ways. War and peace blend."[10]

But Gavin found out that the late 1940s were most inauspicious years to be asking for a "new Army" and radically new equipment. President Truman's secretary of defense, Louis Johnson, favored an austerity program to reduce the armed forces. There would be little in the army budget even for troops, let alone helicopters and STOL airplanes.

The almost frantic demobilization after World War II had reduced the army from 8,268,373 troops in 1945 to 591,487 in 1950. The army budget of nearly fifty billion dollars in 1945 was under four billion by 1950.

General Eisenhower wrote, "The Congress was tired of wartime spending. . . . Even when I went to Capitol Hill, with the President's approval to ask for money with which to collect the Army's usable vehicles scattered across the world, rusting away, so that we could concentrate them in places where they could properly be cared for, my recommendations were ignored."[11]

Such a Congress could hardly be expected to welcome ideas for a new airborne army. Still Gavin felt the military leaders should have fought harder against the dismantling of American military strength. He later included himself "in that group which did not raise a louder cry at this criminal and wasteful destruction of the armed forces."[12]

The Russians, however, had not demobilized to any great extent. In fact they seemed to be expanding everywhere, particularly in Eastern Europe and in Africa and Asia where old Western colonial regimes were toppling.

To meet this expansion, the Truman administration instituted a new policy of "containment." The idea was first publicly proposed in 1947 by George Kennan of the State Department, in an anonymous article in *Foreign Affairs* magazine. "The main element of any United States policy toward the Soviet Union," Kennan wrote, "must be that of a long-term, patient but firm and vigilant containment of Russian expansive tendencies." The hope was that this would eventually force either "the break-up or the gradual mellowing of Soviet power."[13]

Containment was composed of three basic programs: massive economic aid to strengthen Western Europe and to bolster the economies of underdeveloped countries; a series of defense alliances (NATO, in 1949, was the first of these); and a military strategy that would enable the United States to replace a large part of its manpower and conventional weapons with the atomic bomb. The policy required a monopoly of nuclear weapons, a strong strategic air force to deliver them, and the *willingness* to use atomic weapons without hesitation.

Except in Western Europe, the containment policy fell considerably short of success. Gavin and others—including his former commander, General Ridgway— soon saw that the administration's diplomatic position was weakened by lack of any military power, except use of all-out atomic force, which could hardly be applied in such situations as Communist guerrilla insurgency in Greece or Russian pressure on Iran. In 1949 the Russians ended the U.S. monopoly of nuclear weapons by setting off their own atomic bomb, and China became the world's largest Communist state.

Gavin was also in the forefront of another controversy, racial integration. When the all-black 555th Parachute Infantry Battalion (the "Triple Nickels") first came to Fort Bragg from Oregon in late 1945, they forced many of the harsh segregation patterns of pre-war days. They were assigned to a section of the post reserved for "Negro troops," an area romantically named Spring Lake which Gavin later described as a mud pond surrounded by sand. The families of black officers and those of enlisted men entitled to family quarters lived in converted army barracks adjacent to the lake. Rather than pay for this substandard housing, a few enterprising officers installed trailers on the grounds adjacent to the Spring Lake bathing house.

When black officers applying for membership in the main post officers' club never received a reply, the Triple Nickels started their own officers' club in the Spring Lake area. Under the direction of Lt. Forrest Walker of Kansas City, the club soon became a going concern, but it was still a far cry from the main club, with its tennis courts, big ballroom, ample bar, and comfortable furniture. Several of the black officers continued to insist on membership in the larger white club. Finally, in an effort to keep them quiet, the Post Board of Governors granted $60,000 for improvements to the Spring Lake Club.

In the white communities surrounding Fort Bragg, the prejudice took less subtle forms. Buses making the ten-mile trip between Bragg and Fayetteville were clearly labeled "colored." At movie theaters in the town, blacks were restricted to balcony seats only. The Fayetteville police were notorious for their treatment of blacks, sometimes arresting black soldiers for cohabiting with black women. A white soldier in a similar situation was ignored. When Gavin himself protested the injustice of this to the Fayetteville police chief, he received a laugh in reply.[14]

Gavin, more than most officers, sensed the unfairness

of this situation. While he knew he could not change the social system of the whole South, within his own divisional command he moved quickly to provide equal treatment for his black officers and men. Many white officers dragged their feet on desegregation, waiting until the communities where they were stationed were less prejudiced. Gavin felt this was ridiculous—"making the Army a sort of social barometer."[15] He did, however, become involved in local affairs, joining "in order to establish good community relations . . . the Lions Club in the city of Fayetteville, North Carolina. One of the members was the Chief of Police."[16]

At least within the 82nd Division itself, the paratrooper boots and wings of the black soldiers meant a great deal. Paratroopers were still a select group and among them the sense of camaraderie transcended race. It was not uncommon for white and black troopers to socialize together, both on the post and in Fayetteville, then have to separate at the bus station. At the same time, black and white paratroop officers developed a mutual respect. There were few racial incidents of the kind so often found in civilian life.

In March of 1948, Gavin left Fort Bragg and his beloved 82nd Airborne to become chief of staff of the 5th Army in Champaign, Illinois. He and his first wife, Irma, had separated and he was remarried to the former Mrs. Jean Emert Duncan of Knoxville, whom he had met at the officer's club at Fort Bragg. Already a mother of a three-year-old daughter, Caroline, Jean would bear Gavin three more daughters by 1954. She would also become a pillar of strength for him in his difficult and painful battles with the Washington bureaucracy.

A year later Gavin had a new job, in which he felt he might present his ideas more effectively. He was assigned as army member of a weapons Systems Evaluation Group in the Department of Defense, a collection of military officers and civilian scientists and technologists who were to analyze existing weapons and suggest needed changes. He continued to press for a new army in the sky, which he had begun to call "Sky Cavalry." But the administration continued its austerity program and its concept of air and nuclear power with only a small regular army. Through the late 1940s many army units consisted largely of poorly trained replacements. Equipment was not properly maintained, and serious shortages of specialized personnel developed.

Although the new Department of Defense was created in 1949 to make U.S. military planning more efficient, according to Gavin there was still constant inter-service rivalry, bickering, indecision, controversy, turmoil, and frustration. Much of this was caused by failure of our own political-military bureaucracy to plan properly, much due to the cult of personality.[17]

The Air Force seemed to be winning the struggle. Now a separate department within the Department of Defense, it alone could deliver the atomic bomb, the only real option in a major war. And it was in the Air Force that Gavin met much of the opposition to an airborne army. "One early sign came when I wrote an article calling for more 'balanced forces' and criticizing the policy of over-reliance on air power and atomic bombs. I submitted my manuscript to the Defense Department for release, and it was returned with 'non-concurrence' because the Air Force had objected to some passages."[18]

An even bigger problem was that the Department of the Army had agreed to clear all of its requests for air vehicles through the Air Force. In practice, of course, this meant the Air Force could decide what aircraft the army could have. Gavin's plan for an airborne army rested largely on increased use of helicopters, which he had found very versatile in his tests in 1946.[19] He urged that the army procure helicopters, finally discussing it personally with the Director of Requirements of the Air Force. Our discussions were of a rather protracted nature, extending over the better part of a day on the trip that we took through the West Coast aircraft industries. He finally became exasperated with my insistence and said "I am the Director of Requirements and I will determine what is needed and what is not. The helicopter is aerodynamically unsound. It is like lifting oneself by one's boot straps. It is no good as an air vehicle, and I am not going to procure any. No matter what the Army says, I know that it does not need any."[20]

Some army officers, whose thinking was still cast in the mold of World War II, also resisted Gavin's innovations. When he proposed a Sky Cavalry unit to the army staff, the idea was referred to the Armored School at Fort Knox since it was cavalry. Though Gavin foresaw light armored vehicles that could be airlifted to battle, the Armored School thought the idea was too far ahead of its time. The 1972 war game in Einsbaug vindicated Gavin: as many as thirty-four tanks, though protected by nuclear and antiaircraft weapons and jet fighters, were incapacitated for each helicopter.

Defense Secretary Johnson's austerity program continued into 1950, "practically wrecking" the army according to Gavin.[21] On 25 June of that year, a decimated and demoralized army with leftover World War II equipment, and an administration with supreme faith in nuclear bombs to keep the peace, found that North Korean forces with Russian equipment, including T-34 tanks, were invading South Korea. To face this attack, the South Koreans had infantry with not even enough rifles to go around. Because the Soviet Union did not

attend a crucial Security Council meeting and use its
veto power, the United Nations came to South Korea's
aid. But it soon became clear that the United States and
the South Koreans would do most of the fighting. Gen.
Douglas MacArthur, then in Tokyo, was named commander of the U.N. forces.

Gavin arrived in Korea a few weeks before China
entered the war and drove the Americans toward the
sea for the second time. At first Lt. Gen. Walton Walker
of the 8th Army had asked for Gavin as his chief of staff.
Instead, the Department of the Army sent Gavin as a
member of the Weapons Systems Evaluation Group. He
reached Korea in October, along with three civilian
scientists: Dr. Charles Lauriston, Sr., a nuclear physi-
cist; Dr. William Shockley, who would later receive the
Nobel Prize for his work in the development of the
transistor; and Dr. Edward Bowles, who had been scientific advisor to Secretary of War Stimson in World War
II.

Gavin was appalled by and bitter about the ill-pre-
pared and ill-equipped initial forces; the lack of coherent
planning; and, above all, the lack of mobility, for which
he had been fighting so long. He was convinced that
airborne forces could have been first a swift initial
screening and delaying force, then a link between the
invading forces at Inchon and the troops breaking out
from the Pusan Perimeter in the south. It took about two
weeks for these forces to link up. Sky Cavalry, Gavin
argued, could have made this juncture possible within a
few hours. Finally, Sky Cavalry could have prevented
the U.S. forces from stumbling into the Chinese trap in
North Korea in the autumn of 1950. Gavin characterized
American action in Korea as "blundering."[22] By the end
of 1954, he said later,

I felt that we in senior positions in the Army

had to take responsibility for our failure in Korea, that we had failed to convince the Department of Defense that it was impossible to achieve tactical mobility without air mobility and helicopter-type forces.

It is inexcusable for Army officers with the intelligence of my generation to have been surprised by horse cavalry divisions in Korea over a hill a mile away, and have the Second Division cut off and decimated.[23]

The Korean War did produce some changes which pleased Gavin. Secretary of Defense Johnson was fired, and there were technological improvements in jet aircraft. Though helicopters were not used as fully as Gavin wanted, their rescue and evacuation work won them greater respect. Four years later, however, still fighting for Sky Cavalry, he wrote a definitive and outspoken article called "Cavalry, and I Don't Mean Horses," which was published in *Harper's*.[24] Gavin said he "published the article in a civilian magazine first because I doubt that I could have obtained clearance in a military publication, and I had learned the hard way that when one places a manuscript with a civilian editor and he asks for clearance from the Pentagon he is far more likely to have it granted than if a man in uniform asks for it."[25]

In June 1951 Gavin was assigned to Europe as chief of staff in Adm. Robert B. Carney's Southern Command NATO. He used the time to study a part of Europe which most American officers knew little about. In 1952 Gavin was given his last troop command, appointed commanding general of VII Corps, with headquarters at Kelley Barracks, Moehringen, Germany. Headquarters of the 7th Army was twenty minutes away on the other side of Stuttgart. Stuttgart Headquarters, thirty minutes from Kelley Barracks, was the logistical support command for the area.

The principal components of VII Corps were the 28th and 43rd Infantry Divisions, together with assigned armor, engineer, artillery, signal, and mechanized cavalry units. The corps occupied one of the tensest areas in continental Europe, thousands of square miles from the Bavarian Alps in the south to the Russian area in the north, from the French zone in the west to Czechoslovakia on the east. Gavin told young officers newly assigned to his headquarters that their duty was to protect "a lot of real estate . . . against Russian intrusion."[26]

Gavin intended to teach VII Corps, many of whose men had come to Europe expecting a good time, the proper role of a soldier. The GIs found their new commander in their areas before reveille and long after midnight. He could move through a motor pool so quickly that men trying to salute would sometimes be looking at his back before they finished, but even traveling so rapidly he could identify what was combat-ready or what was not. Only a dozen or so years before, he had been a company commander himself.

His weekly staff meetings were designed to educate his staff officers in new tactical fields as well as to discuss immediate concerns. At these meetings, and in briefings following maneuvers, he would interject ideas about the use of helicopters, new electronic weapons, ultraviolet-ray range finders, resupply by air, or strategic uses on a global scale of airborne divisions able to sustain themselves in combat for as long as thirty days. At one such meeting in 1953, preceding German independence and the incorporation of German forces into the NATO framework, Gavin suggested inviting German officers to visit the Corps and exchange thoughts. As various officers voiced their approval, Gavin remarked wryly, "They'd probably tell us we won the war because we had more jeeps than they did."[27]

On his frequent flights over southern Germany, Gavin applied the lessons of military history to the terrain he saw beneath him. Officers accompanying him on these flights found themselves the target of a torrent of questions: What would they do if they found themselves isolated there? How would they plan to receive supplies dropped in their area by C-130s? What would they do if their area was suddenly hit by Russian nuclear weapons?

He stressed concern for the condition and morale of the troop units, which he visited often. After one such visit he remarked that the soldiers were "the truly important ones. As long as we're able to take care of them, we'll be able to get the job done."[28] This attitude was reflected in his continuing involvement with racial integration. In his corps headquarters were a black captain and a black lieutenant in the operations section (G-3), a black major in logistics (G-4), a black sergeant in the personnel section (G-1), and another in the intelligence section (G-2). There was another black major in the inspector general section, and a third was assistant special services officer. In addition, there was an increasing number of black enlisted personnel in supporting units. Despite President Truman's 1948 executive order calling for integration of all armed services, other officers did not match Gavin's record in this area.

Gavin was equally unprejudiced in the social life that he and his wife Jean led. At social functions, Gavin was one of the most active participants, laughing, joking, and dancing. On most evenings, though, the Gavin family retired early, giving the general a chance to catch up on his reading of newspapers, science fiction, politics, poetry, and military history. In superb physical condition and usually requiring little sleep, he could relax so completely that he was quickly ready for the next day's activity.

However, Gavin did not exempt his home life from the general aura of combat-readiness he expected throughout VII Corps, as Jean Gavin and her dinner guests discovered one evening. The Gavins had just sat down at the table with a group of division commanders when the telephone rang, informing the officers of a practice alert. Such drills required that 90 percent of all units leave their barrack areas within a matter of minutes. Gavin himself had scheduled this particular alert and, as always, followed it with a personal inspection of some one outfit's performance.

Still in Germany during the last sterile and wasteful weeks of the Korean conflict, Gavin worried increasingly about the future of the army. The military planner, he believed, "continuously faces criticism from the public, the downgrading of his profession, and sees waste which he could use . . . to accomplish the goals he is charged to meet. Democracies are always proud of the millions they save in peace and they would rather not discuss the billions they waste in war."[29] He realized that in the new missile and nuclear age Americans would no longer have time to prepare while other nations bore the initial brunt of war.

Gavin's military background and training were now as complete as could be expected of any senior general. His brilliant war record, his concepts of tactics and strategy for both conventional and nuclear warfare, and his record with VII Corps had made him one of the most respected officers in the nation's military establishment. In March 1953 he returned to Washington as G-3 (plans and operations) of the Department of the Army. Within two years, he received his third star and, as a lieutenant general, was named deputy chief of plans and research. In October 1955 he became army chief of research and development, with the status of a deputy chief of staff.

But Gavin was to discover that innovation on maneuvers in southern Germany was less irritating to the more orthodox military thinkers than was innovation in the powerful Washington world of budgets, national policy making, and political ambitions.

V. *The Collision Course*

Gavin found a new administration in Washington. Dwight D. Eisenhower, who had taken Gavin's advice on the invasion of Normandy, was now president. Millions of voters had felt that the general who had won the war in Europe could provide the military security America needed at home. Few Americans wanted another war, especially after the bloody debacle in Korea which had been blamed on the Democrats. Eisenhower had also received the support and money of Republican business interests who believed that he would decrease governmental spending, reduce taxes, encourage free enterprise, and balance the budget.

Eisenhower's cabinet reflected the beliefs of his supporters. The new secretary of defense was Charles Erwin Wilson, former president of General Motors Corporation. Beyond the assembly-line production of military hardware, he had little, if any, military or political experience. The new secretary of the treasury,

George M. Humphrey, was a businessman from Ohio. Humphrey was a fiscal conservative whose mission was to cut spending and balance the federal budget. He had enough influence to control decisions that went far beyond money itself. John Foster Dulles, a corporation lawyer, was the new secretary of state. He had been a delegate to the San Francisco Conference of 1945 which had laid the foundations of the United Nations, and had been a U.N. delegate. He was chief architect of the Japanese Peace Treaty in 1951, and from 1950 to 1953 had served as an advisor to the State Department. But Gavin was not sure that Dulles could relate to American foreign policy commitments, nor that he understood the concept of war.

The phenomenon of McCarthyism had further confused America's thinking about defense needs. In 1952 Sen. Joseph McCarthy of Wisconsin had launched a series of sensational investigations into Communism in government and other areas of American life. By 1953, many Americans were so obsessed with fears of suspected Communists among screen writers, actors, broadcasters, and college professors that the real threats from the Kremlin were ignored.

Though helicopters had become more popular and there were increasing numbers of rocket and missile experiments, manned bombers were still a keystone of U.S. defense policy. American planners claimed the Strategic Air Force would be able to use the hydrogen bomb so effectively that it did not matter that the Russians had an H-bomb too.

On 12 January 1954, Secretary of State Dulles spoke at a Council of Foreign Relations dinner at the Hotel Pierre in New York City. He said American foreign policy would be backed up by the "great capacity to retaliate instantly, by means and at places of our choosing" against enemy aggression. He said the

Eisenhower administration would place "more reliance on deterrent power and less dependence on local defensive power."[1] This soon became known as the "massive retaliation" doctrine.

Gavin and many fellow officers realized that reliance on massive retaliation alone would not enable America to cope with the limited ground conflicts it might soon face. Gavin said later, "I had just come back from Nuremberg. What do we do if the Russians decide to occupy it? Do we 'nuclear-liberate' Nuremberg?"[2]

In his first budget message to Congress, President Eisenhower was even more specific than Dulles. For the 1955 fiscal year he proposed a reduction of $5.3 billion in federal spending. While the army's budget would be cut most heavily, the Air Force would receive more money than it had since World War II. This would soon be called the "new look" in America's military establishment, then, for popular appeal, the "bigger bang for the buck."

Secretary of Defense Wilson said in an interview that "the military plans behind the budget represent good planning." He was sure, he said, that the army could carry on its own assignment despite the cuts, and that a strong Air Force would deter any aggressor. "If we do have a war and it develops into a big land engagement," Wilson said, "it would be a pretty sure bet that it would not be on the continental United States." He conceded that America could be attacked by air, but added that the planners had taken into account the "home guard" responsibility of the ground forces.[3]

The chairman of the joint chiefs of staff, Arthur W. Radford, would later argue against Gavin's army missile program by saying that any weapon with a range of over two hundred miles belonged to the Air Force. The Air Force chief of staff was Gen. Nathan Twining, whose service was growing under Eisenhower's "new look" and thus could hardly oppose it. In fact Twining cooperated so well that in 1957 he succeeded Radford as chairman of the joint chiefs. The chief of naval operations was Adm. Robert B. Carney, who quite naturally was looking out for his own branch rather than the ground forces.

However, Army Chief of Staff Gen. Matthew Ridgway not only disagreed with the administration's plans, he spoke out openly against them. As he recalled:

> All these actions which in my view were detrimental to the strength and spirit of the Army I protested in meetings with the Joint Chiefs; in my testimony before committees of Congress; and by letter and in personal conferences with the Secretary of Defense. After each exchange of views with Mr. Wilson, I came away convinced that either his mental processes operated on a level of genius so high I could not grasp his meaning, or that considerations beyond the soldier's comprehension were influencing his thinking. . . . The belief seemed to prevail that it was enough to hold the threat of the A and H bomb over the head of a trembling world. No thinking soldier can accept this view. No honest student of military history could believe that the nuclear bomb alone was that key to quick and easy victory which mankind had sought since wars began.[4]

Another ally of Gavin in the fight against the massive retaliation concept was John F. Kennedy, then senator from Massachusetts. As early as 1954 Kennedy said, "Our reduction of strength for resistance in so-called brushfire wars, while threatening atomic retaliation, had in effect invited expansion by the Communists in areas such as Indochina through those techniques which they deem not sufficiently offensive to induce us to risk the atomic warfare for which we are so ill prepared defensively."[5]

By 1956, Ridgway was retired. His successor as army chief of staff, Gavin's new boss, was Gen. Maxwell D. Taylor, wartime commander of the 101st Airborne Division and Gavin's onetime rival for leadership of the victory parade. That Taylor shared Gavin's distrust of the massive retaliation doctrine is revealed in his later writings. But it was clear from the beginning that he would not speak out as Gavin and Ridgway did. When Taylor was called home from Tokyo where he had been 8th Army commander and supreme commander in the Far East, he was cross-examined carefully by Wilson and Eisenhower. Taylor recalled that "oddly they were not interested in my views on world strategy, but wished to be assured of my willingness to accept and carry out the orders of civilian superiors. . . . In the end I apparently satisfied my questioners."[6]

Between 1953 and 1955 the army's expenditures were cut from about $16.3 billion to $8.8 billion. By 1956 army units as far separated as Hawaii and Georgia were being put together on paper as "divisions." Development of new tactical weapons lagged far behind even Gavin's minimum hopes. Little thought seemed to be given to the limited wars in which massive nuclear retaliation would be impractical or impossible, yet Gavin was convinced that a general war in the atomic age would be a holocaust which no one could win.

He was not advocating abolition of the air force and the H-bomb as deterrents, but he wanted other options as well. Long-range missiles seemed increasingly practical. By the early 1950s several experimental missile programs were underway, but the budget for them was comparatively small. The army's program, Project

Jupiter, was centered at Redstone Arsenal in Huntsville, Alabama. It had the invaluable services of Dr.
Wernher Von Braun and his team of experts, yet Von
Braun credited Gavin himself with much of the development, although he was not a scientist or technologist.[7]

By late 1956, under Gavin's direction as chief of research and development, the Huntsville team had used
a Jupiter-C rocket to fire a small nose cone to an altitude
of 684 miles and a range of 3,355 miles. The experiments
were stopped abruptly by a memo from the Defense
Department which limited the army to a range of two
hundred miles in its tactical surface-to-surface missiles.
No such restrictions were put on either the air force or
navy. Although Eisenhower first supported this limit,
he later approved the army's Pershing missile with a
range of five hundred miles.

Gavin knew the Soviets had a mid-range missile as
early as 1956. All intelligence reports told him that the
Russians were forging ahead in rocketry, and that they
would soon be able to launch a man-made satellite.

The idea fascinated Gavin. In addition to its scientific
research value, the satellite could be a militarily useful
reconnaissance vehicle, not only for individual countries but for international groups such as the United
Nations which helped to maintain peace. For the Soviet
Union to be first in this field, Gavin felt, would be a
"technological Pearl Harbor."[8]

The American satellite development was assigned to
a civilian-directed program called Vanguard, scheduled
to launch a twenty-pound satellite before the end of
1958. Vanguard was based on a completely new missile
development program.

By early 1956, Gavin's army team had developed the
Jupiter-C, with tested and proven components. He was
sure the Jupiter-C could put up a satellite sooner than
Vanguard, and he asked the Defense Department to

consider it. But he was told flatly that the Redstone and Jupiter missiles would not be used to launch a satellite. Evidently the reason for this refusal was that the satellite program was supposed to be peaceful. To involve the army would indicate that the satellite was a new, aggressive weapon. Whatever merit there was to this argument, the Russians drew no such distinction. By mid-1957 it was learned that they had launched a 1,200-mile missile which accurately reached its test target area. Gavin knew then that the Russians had reached outer space, and that their chances of launching a successful satellite during 1957 were very good.

Thus far Congress appeared to have little or no information on the progress of the Soviet missile programs. Was it Gavin's job to sound the alarm? He thought of the young man at Pearl Harbor on 7 December 1941, who first saw the approaching Japanese planes on his radarscope but was told by his superior officer to "forget about it." Should he have bypassed this officer and gone to another? Should Gavin now bypass his superiors? He decided his best course was to ask Maj. Gen. John Medaris, the Huntsville commander, and Dr. Von Braun to investigate the possibility of an interceptor satellite to meet the inevitable Russian challenge.[9]

But in August Soviet Premier Khrushchev stated that the Soviet Union had launched "a super long-distance intercontinental multi-stage ballistic missile."[10] In early September Gavin told a meeting of the Army Scientific Advisory Panel that he believed the Soviets would have a satellite in space within thirty days, and on 4 October his prophecy was fulfilled when Sputnik I went into orbit around the earth.

Americans reacted with wonder, surprise, and fear. Gavin was crushed, but others seemed unaffected. Defense Secretary Wilson said, "We can't afford to fight limited wars. We can only afford to fight a big war, and if there is one, that is the kind it will be." Gavin replied, "If we cannot afford to fight limited wars, then we cannot afford to survive, for that is the kind of war we are confronted with."[11]

Though the American experience in Korea should have made the problem clear to everyone, Gavin still had to point out that "to assume that the Strategic Air Command can deal effectively with every type of limited action is the same as to assume that since a tank battalion can be used to control extensive land areas, one tank can be used to catch a pickpocket or car thief. To win limited wars requires special weapons, equipment and techniques."[12]

VI. *Countdown to Retirement*

Though the Eisenhower administration tried to down-play the launching of Sputnik I, when Sputnik II—with a live dog aboard—was sent into orbit in early November, it was obvious that there was political trouble ahead. Many Americans felt the satellites were a Communist threat, and they saw the man they had elected twice to keep them *ahead* of the Communists had let them fall *behind*. The Democrats, who now had a majority in both houses of Congress, quickly took up the issue and began calling it "the missile gap." Gavin would soon find himself caught up in the political storm.

At the eye of the storm was the senator from Texas, Lyndon Baines Johnson, whom Senator Russell of Georgia had called the Democrats' best hope for the White House in 1960. Johnson had accurately perceived the Republican presidential victories of 1952 and 1956 as won largely through the Cold War appeal of a popular military leader, a vote for security against the Communists. But though Eisenhower had built a mighty Air Force and a mighty bomb, and had even achieved the long-sought balanced budget, the Communists seemed even more menacing. In Sputnik, Johnson saw ammunition he could use against the Republican hero.

By December, Johnson had assembled his Senate Preparedness Subcommittee and a full-scale investigation into Republican defense policies was under way. On the committee's witness list was an impressive array of high-ranking military men, scientists, and industrial leaders: the chiefs of staff of the three services; Dr. Vannevar Bush of the Massachusetts Institute of Technology, a long-time advisor to the military; Adm. Hyman Rickover, the navy's atomic submarine expert; Dr. Von Braun; and others, including Lt. Gen. James Gavin.

All witnesses agreed there was a missile gap. Almost all, even the air force people, said there had not been enough money. Many witnesses said wrong budgetary decisions had been made. The committee wondered if this was due to a poor decision-making system. The hearing began to center on the joint chiefs of staff organization.

When asked his opinion of the organizational structure, Maxwell Taylor admitted that "undoubtedly there are areas in which it seems to me improvement should be sought. But I do not have and am not yet ready to table a solution. I think it takes time and observation and more wisdom than I presently have to come forward with these points. So until I am sure what proposal I would table, I could hardly say what legislation would be required."[1]

Gavin was next. As he entered the senate investigation chamber on Friday, 13 December, he might have recalled the uproar caused by his 1956 testimony on nuclear weapons. Many officers, chastened by such an experience, might have hedged future answers carefully. But Gavin had never found it possible to do this. Still smarting from the Russian "first" in space, he intended to speak out. Too, he knew what no one on the senate subcommittee did, that he was planning to retire from the military. Later he would say that his testimony required no special courage because "I had already burned my bridges behind me."[2]

Because of the ensuing public confusion over Gavin's actions, it is important to note here that all of the bridges had not yet been totally destroyed. It is true that as early as October of 1957 he had made quiet inquiries about what his retirement income would be after thirty years of service. In the weeks before his subcommittee appearance he had had several talks with his boss, Gen. Maxwell Taylor, about his future. Yet, his major goal seems to have been to leave Washington, perhaps as chief of the continental army command. He did not want to continue appearing before Congressional committees and either supporting military policies he believed were dangerous possibly with testimony bordering on perjury, or else risking charges of insubordination by saying what he honestly thought.

He was nearing the end of his fourth year in Washington, the traditional time for reassignment. At each meeting with Taylor, Gavin remembered, "he agreed that I would be reassigned in the near future and in any event that I would not be required to stay more than four years."[3]

The senate hearing probed Gavin's opinions on the missile program. After denying that there had been a lack of money, Gavin attributed America's failure to "wrong decisions." One such decision, he said, had been made in the summer of 1955 when the army's first Jupiter-C proposal had been rejected as the national satellite program in favor of Vanguard. Another mistake came in 1956, when he had again pointed out that Jupiter could launch a satellite sooner than Vanguard, and had again been rebuffed. Later that year, he told the subcommittee, Army Secretary Brucker reopened the issue, again arguing for the army satellite program, but "again it was turned down." The senators later heard the same frustrating story from General Medaris and Dr. Von Braun.

As to limited, or at least nonnuclear, conflict, Gavin claimed the army has been "made, deliberately, impotent to handle that role because of total lack of judgement and inexperience concerning the problems of future warfare." He called for twenty-eight divisions instead of the fifteen then in existence, and said flatly, "I don't believe in next year's budget."

Edwin L. Weisl, the subcommittee's counsel, asked if the basic problem was the organizational setup of the Defense Department. Gavin replied, "I think what really is needed now is a competent military staff of senior military people working directly for the Secretary of Defense. I would have them, and again this is entirely my personal opinion, take over the functions of the Joint Chiefs of Staff. I would have the military staff organized to handle operations, plans, intelligence, and—in fact—break up the Joint Chiefs of Staff."

Weisl turned to Johnson. "You have heard what the General testified to, Mr. Chairman."

"I heard considerable," Johnson replied.[4]

Many witnesses had complained about budget limitations and priorities. But with the exception of Dr. Bush, who also blamed the joint chiefs setup for inter-service "bickering" and lack of a coordinated policy, none had gone quite this far. Gen. Curtis LeMay, the air force deputy chief of staff, had come close when he suggested that eventually the country would need a "single service," with a "single chief of staff, and a single staff to

operate the armed forces." However, he told the senators, "this is a very radical step . . . and I don't think you
can get it right away."[5]

As he expounded on his proposal to break up the joint
chiefs, Gavin said: "The Armed Forces are always accused, or frequently are, of preparing for the last war
rather than the next. I have found to my great disap-
pointment when I have arrived in the position in which
I am supposed to do some of this preparing that it is
exceedingly difficult to get a new idea across. With the
type of professional staff I have recommended, you
would get more understanding, more acceptance, and
as a result better advice going to the Secretary of Defense."[6]

As Gavin concluded his testimony, Johnson leaned
forward and said, "General Gavin, I think I should say
that it has been a real treat to hear you. You talk like the
kind of fellow that I have been looking for ever since we
started these hearings . . . I want to explore further with
you any possible suggestions you might make to us."

Then Johnson added, "Some of the things you said
appear to be not in complete accord with others who
have appeared to date. . . . Do you anticipate any criticism as a result of your very frank response to the
questions that have been propounded to you?"

"No sir," Gavin replied, "I do not."[7]

Was he for once in his life being less than candid? Or
did he still lack political insight? Though the hearings
were closed, his testimony would not long remain secret.
And it would be virtually the last straw to many in both
the civilian and military hierarchies. While naming no
names, Gavin had in fact questioned the whole military
structure and the administration of his commander in
chief.

President Eisenhower made no direct comment on the
testimony, but he was infuriated. His son John believes

that Gavin "exacerbated" the conflict with his father by his appearance before Congress:

> As President, my father resented all this testimony from the various services . . . and he thought the services were not being particularly objective. They were looking out for their own interests . . . . The way it stood was that Congress, for its own purposes, could play one service off against another. And, of course, we had an opposition to Congress.[8]

On 23 December 1957, Gavin was called to the office of Maxwell Taylor for another talk about his future. When Taylor told him that he was to stay on in Washington for another year, Gavin "told him I would submit my request for retirement at once. I did so within an hour."[9] Gavin asked that he be retired 31 March 1958, noting that on that date he would have completed thirty years of service.

The request was addressed to the "Adjutant-General of the Army thru: Chief of Staff, United States Army." First to receive the request was Brig. Gen. William Westmoreland, secretary of General Taylor's general staff. Lt. Gen. (then Lt. Col.) James Sutherland, Gavin's executive officer at the time, later recalled he "handed Westmoreland the sealed envelope and stated that it contained General Gavin's request for retirement. Westmoreland took it, but did not open it during my short stay in his office . . . I heard that he did not open it until some time the following Monday." Sutherland was asked "if I knew of anything that could be done to persuade General Gavin to change his mind . . . I stated that I was personally very sure nothing could be done."[10]

In normal circumstances, such a request would have

been promptly noted with approval or disapproval and
then moved through proper channels. Instead, Westmoreland—without Gavin's consent or knowledge—
locked the request in his safe, hoping that Gavin might
change his mind.[11] Taylor then left for an inspection
tour of the Middle East and Europe. Though Gavin had
felt he had no more decisions to make after submitting
his request,

> it soon became apparent, however, that the
> Administration and Secretary Wilbur Brucker
> were playing some sort of game with me. They
> offered me a fourth star if I would stay, and this
> was to be as commander of the Seventh Army
> in Europe, but this I turned this down. The
> Secretary had several meetings with the Press
> and clearly gave them the impression that I
> was bargaining with him, which I absolutely
> was not. I had no choice in the matter. It was up
> to him to decide what to do. It is my understand-
> ing that the White House did not want me to go
> unscathed as a critic of the Administration. . . . I
> finally told the Senate Committee looking into
> the situation that I would be happy to stay in
> the Army as a private if it were to be the kind of
> Army that I wanted it to be, but that I would not
> stay in it at any grade the way things were
> going. "The way things were going" refers, of
> course, to our policy of exclusive reliance on
> massive retaliation and our neglect of an ade-
> quate space program.[12]

Finally, on 8 January 1958, Gavin's request was delivered to Secretary Brucker. Probably not coincidentally,
three days before the news of Gavin's retirement was
leaked to the press. Sutherland knew that Gavin "had

many friends in the Washington press corps, any one of whom would have been delighted to assist him."[13]

Endorsements on the request show that Gen. Lyman Lemnitzer, acting as chief of staff in Taylor's absence, wrote "recommend approval" and signed it at 2:15 P.M. on 8 January. Secretary Brucker, after three days of being in the embarrassing position of having to admit to the press that he had not yet seen the request, wrote "approved" on the same paper at 3:00 P.M.

Lt. Gen. Donald Booth, army G-1 (personnel) at that time, had talked with Gavin about retirement prior to Gavin's meeting with Taylor on 23 December. Booth felt that Gavin "would shortly be promoted to full general and I also know full well that you would have been Chief of Staff had you stayed in the Army as an active general."[14] Others in Washington, including Lyndon Johnson, felt Gavin had been forced out of the army. The news of Gavin's retirement was hardly out before Johnson announced that he would immediately call Gavin back before his committee.

Without bothering to find out that Gavin had considered retirement long before his 23 December appearance on Capitol Hill, Johnson tried to imply that he was being pressured out of the service because of the testimony on that day. "This committee and its chairman," Johnson said, "are not going to tolerate any Administration rubber-hose tactics or any efforts to put committee witnesses in a straight-jacket." Democratic Senators John Stennis from Mississippi and Stuart Symington from Missouri urged an inquiry into reports that Gavin had been threatened with a transfer to "an obscure post" unless he altered some of his views.

When Gavin reappeared before the senate subcommittee on 8 January, he and Johnson had different goals in mind. Gavin intended to explain his real purpose in leaving the army, while Johnson planned to use him for a new political offensive against the Republican administration. Through a series of carefully planned questions, Johnson led Gavin to give answers that would make it appear he was leaving the service because he had been denied a fourth star, and that this denial was a direct result of his earlier testimony. Johnson "seemed obsessed with the idea that I was being denied a promotion."[15] Then, before the answers could be put into a more accurate context, Johnson began leaking bits and pieces of the testimony to the press.

"It was supposed to be a secret, executive session," Gavin recalled, "and here was Johnson writing notes and giving them to aides who would leave the room with them. Then Johnson himself would get up and leave the session. I could only presume he was talking with others."[16]

Among other things, these premature reports to the press quoted Gavin as saying he was "no longer being considered for promotion and assignment to a more responsible post," and that it did not help a man's career to be "frank and straightforward" in his testimony to Congress. Johnson reported that Gavin said he was told about the "no promotion" decision 23 December by General Taylor. Until then, he said, Gavin believed he was under consideration to become chief of the continental army command. Johnson said Gavin told the senators he could not prove that the decision stemmed from his 13 December testimony, but felt it had something to do with it.

Gavin was not actually misquoted, but not until hours later could his remarks be put in proper context and his real motives for retirement be explained to reporters. Johnson's earlier reports from the committee room made their impact in the afternoon papers and on radio and television. Many people would continue to believe that Gavin was "resigning" because of a blocked promotion.

Further confusion followed when Secretary Brucker, asked about the "no promotion" issue, said Gavin had in fact been offered a fourth star. What apparently was never fully explained was that this star would only come after another year in Washington, a condition Gavin would not accept.

Gavin himself said he was retiring to fight for a better overall national defense. He was naturally especially concerned about the army, "which has a range limit placed on its missiles and a weight limit placed on its planes to face a threat which is increasing in strength. . . . Missiles belong to the Army as much as to any other service. . . . We've got to have the equipment they need."[17]

Throughout January, letters and telegrams supporting Gavin poured into his office at the rate of fifty or more per day. They came from senators, representatives, colleagues, and troopers who had jumped with him from Fort Benning through Sicily, Italy, Normandy, and Holland. Many wanted him to reconsider his decision. Some younger officers wondered why they should stay if Gavin left. While these letters troubled Gavin, he felt many of the messages seemed to have "missed entirely the fundamental principle involved."[18]

He was especially concerned that the "politicians, particularly, seemed unable to grasp the basic facts. Having answered their questions endlessly on The Hill, I am disturbed by their inability to realize that the integrity of oneself must be overriding and may not be compromised, even for the slightest personal gain. . . . The choices, as General [Nathan] Twining recently stated, are apparent: i.e. perjury, insubordination, or 'turning in your suit.' I felt, and still feel, that by retiring I acted in the best interest of the country and the Army, as I see those interests."[19]

Many in the service disagreed with Gavin's position

that he could do more for the nation's defenses out of uniform than in. Gen. Lyman Lemnitzer said later:

> It was obvious to us that General Gavin was extremely frustrated because his views were not being accepted at higher levels, but so were all of us.... He felt he could exercise far greater and more effective influence on the outcome of these policy problems if he were outside the Army and not in it.
>
> We disagreed strongly with his views in this regard.... We considered he was "walking out" on the Army at a very crucial time in the Army's history.... On the other hand, those of us who remained in the Army and continued strongly to oppose over-emphasis on nuclear weapons finally did have a major influence on obtaining decisions and modifications of nuclear and other policies that more clearly conformed to Army views.[20]

Where does one draw the line between honest dissent and insubordination? What restrictions must the military impose in order to function? Is it necessary for the dissenter to "turn in his suit" in order to be fully effective? While Gavin believed some restrictions were necessary, he felt his patriotic duty was to speak directly to his fellow citizens.[21] Even Maj. Alexander de Seversky, a critic of Gavin's limited war theories, agreed with Gavin about military secrecy:

> The current secrecy in the area of defense began immediately after Pearl Harbor, ostensibly to protect secrets from the enemy. But the political and military leaders also found closed doors and censorship a convenient way to hide

their blunders from the American public. . . .
America went into World War II with the P-40,
our primary fighter plane. It was shockingly
inferior. . . . Yet the P-40 was publicly hailed by
the government as the best fighter in the world,
thus shielding those responsible for it from
public reaction.[22]

Throughout the affair of his resignation, Gavin received no personal word from President Eisenhower. As
his State of the Union message to Congress early in 1958
showed, the president had been piqued by the military
witnesses who complained to the Johnson committee.
Gavin felt that direct communication with Eisenhower
might have averted much of the problem.

I didn't expect any special treatment from him.
. . . But what I did expect was a fair and under-
standable hearing of my views, which was not
given to me or to any of us by Wilson as Secretary of Defense. How then can you get these
views to the President when they are blocked by
a secretary of defense who has not the slightest
concept of what you are talking about or what it
means to have an adequate defense program
through missilery and missile warning systems?[23]

There was one dramatic and emotional episode in the
senate hearing room which was not fully reported until
later in 1958. Senator Symington, praising Gavin in a
speech to the St. Louis Chamber of Commerce, quoted
Lyndon Johnson's expression of dismay at Gavin's
retirement: "General, I just think this is a horrible
situation. . . . If men like you, General Gavin—I want you
to listen carefully to these words—if you tuck your tail

and put up the white flag, say 'I can't take it any more' and run from this crowd, we are going to have a second rate Army." Symington also quoted Gavin's reply:

There was some remark entered into the record about tucking one's tail between one's legs and running up the white flag. . . . Let me say we are brought up to do things a certain way in this Army you have created. And I am a product of it. As a matter of fact I came to it a week after my 17th birthday. . . . I was taught things to do there. . . to seek danger because that is where the decision is made. . . . I took three thousand troopers into Sicily, and left a lot of them there. . . . Then I went up to London to advise General Eisenhower as an airborne advisor, and we planned the Normandy operation. I asked to go back to my outfit. . . . This is where the danger, that is where the decisions were made, and that is where I was brought up to go. . . . Then we had the promise of peace. I have been trained in peace, above all, to be honest, to be cooperative with my fellow servicemen, and to obey my civilian superiors. . . . I don't want promotion. I want to be honest with myself. I want to serve my country the way I have been brought up, to walk into danger. That is why I am here. I asked to go to this committee because I thought that is where the decisions are going to be made to affect the security of this country. I am here for that reason.[24]

VII. *The New Career*

On the afternoon of 31 March 1958, Lt. Gen. James M. Gavin (USA Retired) walked out of his office suite in the Pentagon Building for the final drive to his quarters at Ft. Myer, Virginia. There was no gala farewell party. Still, things could have been worse. Six months earlier, when he had made quiet inquiries about what his retirement income would be after thirty years' service, he had been startled to find that it would be only a little more than $500 a month. When he finally left the Pentagon, however, Gavin's financial future had brightened considerably.

> I received about 90 offers from industries all over the country. I was amazed, because I had been quite sure that I would not get any suitable job, and I did have a lot of girls to get through school. Some of the best offers appeared to be from the aerospace industry, notably Lock-

heed, Westinghouse, and Food Machinery Corporation.

Henry Kissinger talked to me about going up to Harvard to join him as a Fellow at his Center for International Affairs. Professor Strausz-Hupe asked me to join him at the University of Pennsylvania in Philadelphia in a somewhat similar role. I remember Arthur Hadley suggesting to me that I spend a year on the Yale campus just to put my thoughts together, etc. I received a positive query from Royal Little in the name of Arthur D. Little, Inc.[1]

Arthur D. Little, Inc. (ADL) was then a comparatively small research and consulting firm with an annual business of about $12 million, almost all of it in the United States. In 1886 Little, a young chemistry student from the Massachusetts Institute of Technology, had gone into business on the Boston waterfront analyzing and evaluating imports for merchants who wanted to make sure they were getting what they paid for. The consulting business was formally organized in 1909.

The company had soon turned to a variety of new projects. In 1911 it aided General Motors in forming its first central research department. In 1916 it directed a survey of natural resources in Canada for the Canadian Pacific Railroad. In World War I ADL worked on the development of new gas mask filters and airplane dopes. In 1921, in an effort to draw more public attention to the possibilities of research and chemistry, Little himself confounded the proverb by making a silk purse out of sows' ears. (The purse finally found its way to the Smithsonian Institution.) In World War II ADL helped develop a device for converting salt water to fresh water, which became standard equipment on U.S. submarines.

Nevertheless, the company did not grow spectacularly. From a staff of twenty in 1909 it had expanded to only about a hundred people by World War II. After the war its growth increased somewhat, with new research on liquid fuel systems for rockets, and a new Management Services Division to help business managers cope with new technology. At the same time it made a few ventures overseas, first conducting studies for Puerto Rico's economic development program—Operation Bootstrap—and later similar projects in Egypt, Iraq, and the Philippines.

When it offered Gavin a job, ADL was still far from the big company it would later become, and the vast majority of its business was still confined to the United States. But Gavin was impressed by the staff, and liked the fact that ADL "had practically no government business."[2] He felt it was important to avoid the appearance of a conflict of interests, since he expected to be outspoken in his criticism of the military. At first he hoped to "combine both the Center for International Affairs at Harvard and ADL. I underestimated the demands that ADL would make on my time and within a month or so it was clear that I could not serve both institutions, so I concentrated on ADL."[3]

Impressed as Gavin was with the ADL staff, the feeling was not immediately mutual. Before he was hired, he was asked to meet with eight of the company's senior managers. The men suspected that Gavin was being considered as a potential president, and some of them "were quite hostile. I guess all of them thought that they themselves should have been nominated to become president of the company."[4]

The session began at 9:00 A.M. and was scheduled to run through lunch. But by late in the morning, the questions were tapering off. Finally, Dr. Larry Bass asked Gavin his opinion of Suetonius. Fortunately, only a year or so earlier Gavin had read Suetonius, the biographer whose work includes many racy tales about the exotic sexual tastes of the Roman emperors. Gavin replied, "I think that he should be published in paper-back, with a picture of a naked woman on the cover. It would be a best seller."[5] Though some members of the group seemed puzzled by this exchange, Bass obviously thought the answer was fine and the atmosphere of hostility soon disappeared.

Gavin accepted the ADL offer of a job as vice-president for management and operations. He would report for work in Cambridge in mid-1958. Meanwhile, he, Jean, and the children would go to Southern Pines, North Carolina, for a well-earned rest.

In the final days of Gavin's military career, Jean had shared his problems and his pains. She had been especially angered by Lyndon Johnson's premature press statements which led many to believe Gavin was bargaining for a fourth star. But she had faced the situation bravely. In a magazine article written shortly after Gavin's retirement she said, "When I married Jim I knew that we would not have an easy life, considering his views, his outspokenness, and his desire to do many things for the service which had not been done before. I knew he faced opposition, and that the road was not all peaches and cream."[6]

At the time of their move to Cambridge, the Gavins had four young daughters: Caroline, aged twelve; Patricia, eight; Aileen, six; and Chloe, three. Jean was particularly concerned about their education. She felt the school system at Ft. Myer had been less than satisfactory, and had caused some basic reading problems which required special tutoring. Patricia had an additional disadvantage. When she was first learning to talk the Gavins had lived in Italy and Germany, and Patricia had been surrounded by non-English-speaking people, especially housemaids.

Jean Gavin always tried to keep the children free of any special pressures as the daughters of a famous man. In fact, all four girls caught up quickly in school, and eventually all became college graduates: Caroline from Vassar with a major in psychology; Patricia from the University of Miami in art history; Aileen from Boston College in sociology; Chloe from Harvard in Russian history and literature.

Gavin reported for work at the Arthur D. Little Company in June 1958. Ray Stevens, then ADL president, was nearing retirement, as was Earl Stevenson, chairman of the board of directors. Gavin was viewed as the most likely candidate to move into Stevens's job, and from there probably into Stevenson's.

Nick Denninger, later to become an ADL vice-president, was aware of concern among the staff when the announcement was made that a retired, controversial general was headed for a top position in the company. It was the first time in ADL history that an outsider had been so appointed. From 1909 to 1936, Arthur D. Little himself, a "structured and somewhat conservative figure," had run the firm. Then, until 1956, Earl Stevenson had been president, supervising the company with "somewhat of a paternalistic hand."[7]

Dr. Cyril C. Herrmann, a young ADL vice-president in economic development work who would soon become one of Gavin's closest associates, felt that Stevenson's popularity during his twenty years at the top of the company made Gavin's position more difficult. The selection of Gavin from the outside was not taken "as any great compliment to the internal staff of ADL," a place where "everyone thought he could become president."[8]

Also, ADL employees had followed the press reports of Gavin's disagreements with Secretary of Defense Wilson. Some had formed an image of an obstreperous general who might be hard to get along with. Yet another handicap was Gavin's background, military rather than academic. However, the staff was after all "research-oriented in our point of view. We decided that we would not polarize our attitude, but rather try to discover the truth of the situation as it might be revealed."[9]

Gavin's first assignment at ADL was hardly prestigious, at least in the eyes of most of the staff. He was to head a recently organized Management Services Division, which was still not considered of any real importance by ADL scientists and engineers. At the same time there was considerable controversy within the division itself as to its role and its future. Some members of the staff wanted to leave ADL and organize a competitive company of their own. Strong personalities among the employees exacerbated the touchy situation.

At first Ray Stevens, the ADL president, did not plan to put Gavin into management services. He seemed to want "to keep me above all that turbulence in preparation for taking over as president." When Gavin finally asked to take over the division, several of his new acquaintances at ADL warned him against accepting. One said, "don't touch it with a ten-foot pole."[10]

But Gavin rejected the advice. He attributed his initial success to the close professional support of Dr. Herrmann and another associate in the division, Harry Wissman. Herrmann became Gavin's marketing and sales manager; Wissman, a graduate of the Harvard Business School who had joined ADL in 1928, was asked to serve as business and financial manager.

The image of the blustering general soon faded. Instead, the ADL people found "perhaps the most skilled professional in the planning process that has ever been a member of the ADL family."[11] Gavin initiated a series of long-range planning meetings on the future of the

Management Services Division, though at that time any formal effort to determine the future of a division at ADL was quite unusual. "We even accepted the hypothesis," Herrmann remembered, "that in a consulting firm you can't really plan for the future. Conditions change rapidly and you have to be responsive to these changes. I believe we have long since abandoned that view, but that was what Gavin encountered."

Herrmann believed that Gavin's wartime experience—"planning at the very highest levels"—helped equip him for this ADL role. Gavin "was experienced in coordinating far more complex sets of variables in the planning process than any of the internal managers within ADL. . . . And it was this planning capacity that won him the respect of the staff."[12]

Gavin's personal warmth also contributed to his success with the ADL staff. When one of Gavin's former sergeants came by to visit him and was told by a secretary that the general was too busy to see him, Gavin quietly rebuked the secretary and sent Denninger to Boston to try to find the sergeant. The ADL staff learned that Gavin did not fit "the stereotype of the military flag officer model. Whether that stereotype is true is another question, but he certainly didn't fit it."[13] And Gavin had an "ambassador" at ADL before he arrived—George Kimball, a senior staff member in the operations research group who had worked with Gavin when they were both members of the Weapons Evaluation Group at the Pentagon.

When he first arrived, Gavin found ADL "in very tight financial straits." It did not seem to be growing to meet the challenges of new competition. Gavin knew that they "had to go out and sell. We had to grow to live."[14] Foreseeing that much of this growth would have to be overseas, Gavin sent Herrmann to Europe, to make a study of how to establish Arthur D. Little. . . . I followed the research procedure of ADL to cover England, Belgium, France, Holland and Switzerland. . . . My recommendations included setting up an initial office in Switzerland, putting a second office in London, as soon thereafter as possible, and a third office in Brussels where the newly established European Common Market was just getting under way.

The report that I submitted to General Gavin . . . engendered a considerable amount of discussion. At such a point it would have been easy for the report to flounder and to be put on the shelf. General Gavin did not permit this to happen. It was very much a function of his own personal leadership that we went ahead very promptly and established our first office in Zurich. . . . By the mid-sixties we had an office in Paris and soon after that another in Heidelburg and then Athens and most recently, Madrid. . . . By the time of the oil crisis of the mid-seventies, ADL was already well established in the Middle East. . . . Once again, this demonstrates the ability of General Gavin to sense what lies ahead. . . . In assessing the successes of General Gavin at Arthur D. Little, I believe that I would put his expansion of our firm into being a multinational company at the top of the list. Was it difficult to do? Yes, indeed. . . . [And Gavin] was one of the first . . . to realize how [telecommunications] would revolutionize our lives.[15]

Advancing rapidly to executive vice-president and a member of the board of directors, Gavin became a major force in ADL's massive expansion program. By 1960 its staff was spread from Europe to Latin America and Canada, and numbered nearly fifteen hundred. In March of that year Gavin was elected president of the company.

Today many at ADL regard the internationalization of the company as Gavin's biggest single achievement. At the time, however, there were some who questioned the policy. According to John Magee, ADL "is not a company that accepts authority or accepts conclusions." Gavin's success in getting his international expansion plan accepted was "substantially one of facilitating, supporting, encouraging and helping; he did not dictate it. I know he was intelligent enough to know that if he dictated it it wouldn't have happened."[16]

Cyril Herrmann believed it was precisely because Gavin was not dictatorial that he was successful in dealing with the staff of a professional research firm. Herrmann recalled that "it was very difficult to remember that he was indeed a famous general. In all the years I worked with him I never heard him raise his voice in anger or frustration. As a matter of fact, when he was really being emphatic he tended to lower his voice."[17]

Gavin's knowledge of the foreign scene, acquired through his years of duty in Europe, also contributed to his success in internationalizing ADL. From the beginning he "was in constant touch with high level company officials, none of these having the capabilities or credentials to compare with his in the foreign scene— knowing the countries, his personal touch with foreign officials and foreign business people. Jim had a flair for that. He liked them and they liked him."[18]

The early months at ADL were a busy time for a man supposedly "retired." But Gavin had also promised to carry on his fight for a better national defense. In late 1958 he published his second full-length book, *War and Peace in the Space Age*. Much of it is a recital of his battles against the massive retaliation policy of the Eisenhower administration. He also predicted that "manned space vehicles will be in orbit by 1965. . . . It is past time, therefore, that we give thought to an organization to conduct space exploration. . . . A command must be organized now to study the problem of space flight, and the strategies and tactics of space combat."[19]

He recommended that the new space command be unified, with all services reporting directly to the secretary of defense. He hoped that by then the joint chiefs of staff would have been abolished.[20]

Among those who reviewed the book was Sen. John F. Kennedy. He described it as a "somewhat hasty, but nonetheless incisive and panoramic review of our defense position during the decade just past and the decade ahead." He added:

> There are two inescapable conclusions that emerge from a reading of this book; first, there is a dangerous military gap between the overall capabilities of the United States and the Soviet Union that will steadily widen in the next five years, particularly in the long range missiles; second, that this gap was not inevitable and was largely produced by actions taken since 1953. . . . Secretary Wilson, who departed from office with an aura of being the shrewd and honest administrator, is depicted—with ample documentation—as a bullheaded and misinformed man who misled both himself and the President with his notions of defense on the cheap.[21]

Elected president in 1960, Kennedy proposed making Gavin head of the National Aeronautics and Space Agency. But Vice-President Lyndon Johnson argued that it would be a serious mistake to appoint any military man to head NASA. As Johnson later recalled:

> I reminded him of the great debate and searching inquiry we had gone through at the time the Space Act was passed, before we finally resolved that the space program should be civilian controlled. To put a military man in charge at this juncture, I feared, would make other nations uneasy, would dim the image of peaceful development we had carefully created. ... President Kennedy said in effect: "All right, find another administrator."[22]

The NASA job went to James Webb, a former director of the budget and under secretary of state during the Truman administration. Gavin, however, was not forgotten. Kennedy wanted to talk with him personally about a very different job, that of U.S. ambassador to France.

VIII. *Ambassador to the Court of de Gaulle*

"Jim," the president said, "are you going to help me with this damn thing or not?"

"Of course I'm willing to help, Mr. President," Gavin replied, "but I think there are people more qualified than I. . . ."[1]

What was troubling newly elected President John F. Kennedy was how to establish better relations with France—especially with its imperious President Charles de Gaulle, whose anti-Americanism was by now well known and feared as a threat to the NATO alliance.

Kennedy felt that Gavin, as ambassador to France, could help cool the situation. Gavin pointed out that he had no formal diplomatic experience and that he did not even speak French very well. But Kennedy told Gavin "with your background in the Army, your being a maverick, an independent thinker, and an innovator, your career parallels de Gaulle's. . . . You knew de Gaulle in London, you landed in Normandy, you played a fine role in helping free France from German control. . . ."[2]

Gavin had hoped that if he were offered a post in the new administration it would be as secretary of defense or chairman of the Atomic Energy Commission. He knew that his appointment as ambassador might be opposed by Charles Bohlen, assistant secretary of state, who had himself wanted the Paris assignment. Another problem was Gavin's commitment to the Arthur D. Little Corporation, of which he had just been made president.

He asked Kennedy for some time to decide. Back in Boston he talked it over with Jean, and after "much soul searching . . . we felt that it was in the best interests of the country. There was a tremendous job to be done over there and if I could contribute to the solution of the problems between our countries I'd be happy to address myself to the work."[3] The directors of ADL agreed to give Gavin a leave for eighteen months at two-thirds of his annual pay, about $60,000. After that, he would be on his own financially until he returned. He accepted Kennedy's offer on the understanding that he would spend no more than two years in France. He wanted to return to ADL reasonably quickly, to resume work on the new programs he had just begun.

The reaction to Gavin's appointment was mixed. In his column of 7 February 1961, James Reston listed several of Kennedy's new ambassadors who "certainly do not meet his test of the 'best available'." Among these was "Gen. Gavin, a distinguished soldier, who is going to Paris with a smattering of tourist French (after all Kennedy said about the importance of language)."[4] *Time* said it appeared that Kennedy was trying to "match one obstreperous General with another."[5] Walter Lippmann found the appointment "unpromising at first glance." However, Lippmann added, "these two

generals have a common language in that both possess
what is so rare in the armed services, truly inquiring,
original minds. Both are insiders in the military profession with brilliant military experience. But they are not
conventional and conformists, and they are not overly
impressed by the big brass. It is not impossible that
between them they may work out for NATO that new
military doctrine which it sorely needs."[6]

Gavin found that almost everyone in the State Department was opposed to de Gaulle. The haughty
French president's drive for a revival of French power
and influence in world affairs had caused both irrita-
tion and concern. France was the logistical base for the
North Atlantic Treaty Organization, and a prepon-
derence of NATO and U.S. forces were based there.
Many in Washington feared that a strong France,
under a strong, independent thinker like de Gaulle,
would not be sympathetic to U.S. interests in Western
Europe. The French had already tested their own atomic bomb in the north African desert, and de Gaulle was
openly planning his own nuclear force despite U.S.
opposition.

Many Americans felt de Gaulle was ungrateful to be
so anti-American after the United States had aided
France in two world wars and spent billions of dollars in
economic aid to the country after World War II. De
Gaulle would soon anger them even more by saying that
France not only needed no more American aid, but
could send some aid to the U.S.

Gavin discovered that officials in the State Department hoped de Gaulle would not be in power long. After
all, since World War II the French had gone through
more than twenty governments. Gavin was disturbed to
realize that "our own State Department [was] in a posture opposite to Kennedy's."[7]

Among those Gavin contacted in his rounds of the

State Department was Charles Bohlen, who later succeeded him in the Paris office. Gavin told him "that
upon my departure from the post—within two years—I
would recommend him for the job. I had hoped this
would smooth his ruffled feathers and enable both of us
to help the President achieve his goal of establishing
better rapport with de Gaulle . . . but I don't think this
helped. Whenever I came back to Mr. Bohlen I found
him cold and not receptive to whatever good I had to say
about de Gaulle."[8] Gavin felt that Bohlen's continued
hostility to de Gaulle impaired the former's usefulness
when he became ambassador in 1963.

Gavin arrived in Paris with his family on 22 March
1961. Most inauspiciously his train overshot the recep-
tion platform and protocol officials and diplomats had
to run after it, pushing their way through crowds of
onlookers and photographers to greet the new ambassador. Despite all this, the welcoming party responded
with warm applause. Gavin presented his credentials to
de Gaulle soon after, and soon the fifty-three-year-old
maverick American general and the seventy-year-old
maverick French president were on much better terms
than the State Department had expected. As Kennedy
had perceived, they had much in common. Both had
been military commanders as well as military critics,
had fought the establishment for new ideas and better
defenses. Both were innovators and intellectuals.

But the cordiality between de Gaulle and Gavin was
based on considerably more than this. First, Gavin had
not come to Paris fearing, as his State Department
superiors did, a strong France. The challenge as he saw
it, was to promote friendship between the U.S. and its
allies. Gavin understood why de Gaulle was behaving
as he did, and he was not unsympathetic. When the
aging French general left retirement in mid-1958 to take
the leadership of the Fourth Republic, France had suf-

The chief of army research and development with a model of the Jupiter missile, summer 1957.

Senator Johnson and Gavin confer at the opening of Congress, 1958.
Hank Walker. © Time Inc. 1958.

As marshal of the inaugural parade, Gavin stands between Mrs. Kennedy and the new president. Truman, in the top hat, is behind Johnson. *Art Richerby.* © Time Inc. 1961.

The president of Arthur D. Little, Inc. at home with his family, February 1961. Left to right: Patricia, Chloe, Gavin, Mrs. Gavin, Caroline, Aileen. Wide World Photos.

President Kennedy and his new ambassador to France consult in the White House 9 March 1961, before Gavin leaves for his post in Paris. Wide World Photos.

Ambassador Gavin presents his credentials to President de Gaulle.

Attorney General Robert Kennedy, Gavin, and President Johnson meet at the White House, 12 June 1964. Wide World Photos.

Right: The chairman of ADL in the early 1970s.

Gavin and Mrs. Gavin at a formal function in Boston, 1978.

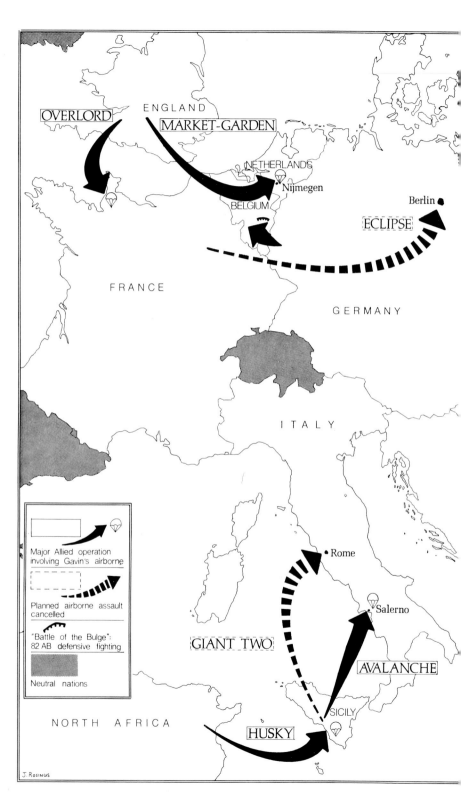

OVERLORD

ENGLAND

MARKET-GARDEN

NETHERLANDS
Nijmegen

BELGIUM

Berlin

ECLIPSE

FRANCE

GERMANY

ITALY

Rome

Salerno

GIANT TWO

AVALANCHE

SICILY

HUSKY

NORTH AFRICA

Major Allied operation
involving Gavin's airborne

Planned airborne assault
cancelled

"Battle of the Bulge":
82 AB defensive fighting

Neutral nations

J. ROSINUS

fered a series of severe setbacks. It had lost its empire in
Indochina after a bloody colonial war. Morocco and
Tunisia had broken away in Africa. A long, costly war
in Algeria was straining the French economy and causing increasing dissension in France. The country
seemed almost paralyzed by internal political bickering, and was powerless to play any real role in the
reconstruction of Europe.

De Gaulle set out to remake France into a first-rate
power, economically as well as militarily. But at the
same time, the U.S. was asking France to continue as
sort of junior partner among the Western powers, with
its defense forces integrated into a NATO clearly dominated by America. Gavin realized this was a position de
Gaulle could not accept if he hoped to restore French
pride and confidence. When in 1958 de Gaulle had proposed to President Eisenhower and British Prime Min-
ister Macmillan an arrangement whereby a Western
Big Three would coordinate global strategy, his plan
was flatly rejected. De Gaulle would never forget the
rebuff, which strengthened his determination to be independent.

While Gavin worked for better French-American relations, Jean discovered there was a vast difference
between being an army wife and the wife of an ambassador in a foreign country, especially when one is not
fluent in the language. Fortunately she was able to
establish a good relationship with Mrs. de Gaulle. CBS
correspondent Charles Collingwood, who knew both
the de Gaulles and the Gavins well, felt that "Mrs. de
Gaulle liked Jean very much."[9] Despite her popularity
in the French diplomatic circle, Jean worried about her
family life as her duties often took her away from the
children.[10]

Living costs were high in Paris, especially the price of
clothing. While Jean had formerly made many of the

children's clothes herself, there was little time for this economy now and she had to have additional clothing sent from the United States. Gavin soon came to understand why people of independent wealth were often chosen for ambassadorial jobs, even though he felt this should not be the main criterion.

As ambassador Gavin dealt directly with President de Gaulle, whom he liked personally. Describing him as "one of the giants of our time," Gavin said, "if there were anything in his makeup that would not appear entirely right, it was the fact that he saw the world in power circles in which France, the United States, and Russia would be the controlling powers, and that these three nations should meet and decide what was best for the rest of the world."[11]

At the heart of American problems with France, Gavin knew, were military differences—especially over de Gaulle's plan to develop his own nuclear force. Many in Washington felt this French effort was foolish, dangerous militarily, and injudicious economically. Moreover, the critics said, it would be impossible for France ever to develop a nuclear force competitive with those of the United States and the Soviet Union.

By 1962 de Gaulle's independent stance would bring him into conflict with Secretary of Defense Robert S. McNamara. When he first came to Washington in 1961, McNamara began to reevaluate U.S. nuclear policy. Like Gavin, he saw the Dulles-Wilson doctrine of massive retaliation as too inflexible. He set up study groups to reorganize the Pentagon and come up with new policies. Within a year, the massive retaliation policy was replaced with a new one called "unified deterrence." In a June 1962 speech at Ann Arbor, Michigan, McNamara said:

There must not be competing and conflicting

> strategies to meet the contingency of nuclear war. . . . If, despite all our efforts, nuclear war should occur, our best hope lies in conducting a centrally controlled campaign against all of the enemy's vital nuclear capabilities. . . . Limited nuclear capabilities operating independently are dangerous, expensive, prone to obsolescence, and lacking in credibility as a deterrent.[12]

Though there was no direct mention of France in the speech, de Gaulle saw that McNamara opposed his desire to become a member of the Big Three Western nuclear club. The French felt McNamara was saying "let the French fight on the ground and the U.S. will handle the nuclear umbrella and the air warfare."[13]

But Gavin also worried that McNamara and the Defense Department were making foreign policy, while the State Department followed their lead. Gavin would learn that copies of his own messages to the State Department were being carefully scrutinized by the military both in France and at home.[14]

While Gavin recommended that the United States sell nuclear energy to France for the same price and on the same basis as to England, and accept de Gaulle's desires for nuclear parity or recognition, the State Department disagreed. Military men having access to Gavin's cables would then support the State Department's position, second-guessing the recommendations of the ambassador who was the representative of the president. Gavin later viewed such tactics as the beginning of a "militarization" of foreign policy which would ultimately lead the nation into the morass of Vietnam.[15]

Gavin believed that de Gaulle never thought of a French nuclear force in terms of the actual circumstances in which it might be used, nor did he envision a

situation in which French nuclear weapons alone would
have to deter a superpower in any future confrontation.
French nuclearization, he felt, was pursued to supple-
ment American capability, to give France some independent military latitude, and above all, to make her
more believable as a world power. He believed

> that French pride was a key issue. She had
> recently lost costly wars in Algeria and Viet-
> nam which signified the end of a once-great
> colonial empire. She had to reconcile the Army
> to this loss and at the same time restore confi-
> dence in her destiny.... Were Great Britain and
> Germany allowed to achieve a monopoly of
> atomic technology in Europe, France would not
> be in any position to significantly affect Euro-
> pean policy.[16]

Despite Gavin's views, Kennedy increasingly listened to Robert McNamara. Gavin became frustrated
with the lack of coordination in developing a policy for
dealing with de Gaulle. He had expected diplomatic
leadership from the State Department, but little was
forthcoming. Though he knew that military education
included economics, geopolitics, and international relations, he did not feel it necessarily produced experienced
political experts capable of understanding the sub-
tleties of diplomacy. Likewise, while McNamara and
his study groups were paragons of efficiency and com-
puterized international planning, they were not equipped to perceive the complex human problem involved in
American relations with France. His beliefs were supported by one confrontation in 1962 between de Gaulle
and Gen. Lauris Norstad, NATO commander. As Gavin
recalled the confrontation,

Norstad wanted to place fighter bombers on bases in France and I think they were carrying nuclear weapons. De Gaulle stipulated something about wanting to know where and how many and what it was and so on, and Norstad stood up to him and said, in effect "I won't tell you." De Gaulle said okay, you don't come in.[17]

Gavin came home in late 1962. He had fulfilled his promise, and was anxious to get back to Arthur D. Little and his real love, research, serving the country on a broader basis. He had established a warm personal relationship with de Gaulle that was to continue for many years. When he called on the de Gaulle family on later visits to France, he was always welcomed as both a friend and colleague.

As ambassador, Gavin had at least thawed the chilly French attitude toward the United States and had improved relations between the two presidents. When John Kennedy visited France in 1961, he was warmly welcomed and had a pleasant visit with de Gaulle, though no new ground was broken. Gavin's successor, Charles Bohlen, lacked Gavin's rapport with de Gaulle. Kennedy's efforts to encourage friendship between the two countries ended with his assassination in the autumn of 1963, and by 1966 de Gaulle had ejected all U.S. troops from French soil.

It is probably safe to say that during his time in Paris Gavin learned more about the U.S. State Department than he did about the French. As usual, he was vocal with his criticisms. In long conversations with President Kennedy, he said the department, which should be "our first line of defense" in international affairs, was too weak. It lacked organization and trained personnel. The Defense Department made a more impressive showing and thus, even when wrong, its views were accepted.[18]

Gavin felt the diplomatic corps was not as well trained as the armed forces. He was "convinced that the first thing we have to do at the State Department is to get about a thousand more foreign service officers and at once begin to send those who are already career officers back to school, for masters' degrees and doctorates . . . I know it would take a generation to really do this, but in time we'd upgrade the Department to where it could do good, effective creative thinking." He believed such an educational program would enable the department "to perform its role without undue military influence and pressures."[19]

While Gavin's lifelong hunger and respect for learning may have led him to overestimate the value of advanced college degrees in demilitarizing U.S. foreign policy, "John Kennedy was very worried about the State Department. In fact, about a week before his assassination I had a long talk with him and he said, 'Well, the General [de Gaulle] is coming over in another month or so, but first I've got to get that State Department straightened out.' . . . But with the assassination all that came to an end."[20]

IX. *Back at ADL*

Months before he left Paris, Gavin knew that the Arthur
D. Little Company was having problems. Both the opportunities and the competition in the consulting and
research fields were mushrooming, and ADL was simply not growing fast enough to meet them. "A senior
member of the staff told me in mid-1962," Gavin later
recalled, "that if I didn't get back soon the company was
going to be in serious trouble. I asked John Kennedy to
let me come back in October. ... He and I knew then that
his problems were not in France, but in the State Department."[1]

During Gavin's absence ADL's former president, Ray
Stevens, had come back from retirement to take his
place. As always, Stevens managed to keep things running and tried to make progress. Nevertheless he was
handicapped by the fact that he did not want to institute
any new policies or interfere in any way with Gavin's
return. When Gavin resumed the presidency, Stevens

returned happily to retirement. There were no conflicts of authority between the two men.[2]

Back at the helm of ADL, Gavin renewed his drive for overseas consulting business. The company's future work would include date processing and marketing in Algeria, beef cattle distribution in Colombia, plywood and veneer processing in Nigeria, and liquified natural gas in the Middle East.

At home, the growing number of urban development projects and an increasing concern for the environment would bring large contracts from both government and private clients, such as a $50 million renewal program for East Cleveland, a new truck transportation system for Dallas, and the environmental impact of a proposed new airport in St. Louis. In research the variety was endless—from cigarette filters to thermal probes of the moon, from cancer chemotherapy to finding out how to make margarine taste more like butter, from pesticides to the future of nuclear energy.

At the same time, ADL became increasingly involved in helping blacks and other minority groups develop their own businesses and industries. It moved quickly on its own affirmative action program to open up new opportunities for minority people within ADL itself. When Cyril Herrmann "was made a vice-president in 1957 I was the first Roman Catholic to become an officer of Arthur D. Little. To move within a few years toward the Affirmative Action program set for us by General Gavin was quite revolutionary."[3]

When Gavin returned to ADL in 1962, he realized much business was available. New technology was expanding so rapidly that most industries needed outside help to keep up. There were dozens of nations formed after World War II that were anxious for development and expertise. The need to rebuild American cities was obvious, and there was an increasing flow of federal funds to get new programs underway.

But to share fully in the market ADL first needed money to expand. "I learned from experience," Gavin said later, "that ADL's potential for growth was severely limited by its lack of capital. It was a serious problem, and no one knew how to grapple with it."[4] The special committee which Gavin organized found no way for the company to acquire additional capital as a basis for growth.

Gavin's next move was to appoint a new corporate treasurer, Paul Littlefield. While this tightening of purse strings helped, the final answer came in 1969 when ADL sold stock shares which until then had been held by the company's pension fund. Gavin remembered the sale was "a traumatic experience for everyone, including me. . . . But, looking around at the competition—McKinsey, Booz-Allen, Stanford Research—it was obvious that I was going to have to find some way to get money and shares for acquisitions and growth."[5]

During the early Gavin years the company sometimes seemed like more of a "club" than a business firm. Many, if not most, of the ADL people strongly opposed the idea of selling the stock, of spreading this family of scholars and scientists into the public financial domain. The trustees, however, agreed with Gavin, who did not "know when I have done as much soul-searching over a problem."[6]

Going public did help ADL to grow, after a two-year recession. But Gavin felt an even more important ingredient in the company's success story was its "absolute integrity." He once told an interviewer that if ADL made automobiles, "we would want them to be perfect. But we don't make things, and we have to earn a reputation for very high professional competence and honesty in everything we do. If we have to tell a client that something he wants very much to do just won't work, we know we are making him unhappy, but we still must say it."[7]

Gavin was careful to assign a project "to the individuals best qualified to handle it. Pay no attention to hierarchy."[8] He knew the importance of making himself visible to his employees and made more visits to the San Francisco office, for instance, than any other officer of the company. On these western trips he always found time to visit one of the campuses of the University of California, to talk with faculty specialists in various fields, and to talk with the students. Herrmann felt this contact with students helped keep Gavin

> in the mainstream of new thinking. . . . Never once did I ever find him on the side of an issue that could be described as being "behind the times" or espousing the viewpoint of "the older generation." Somehow he had the intuitive ability to keep abreast of things and to know how things are changing. An important part of this ability is rooted in his interest in and respect for the views of young people.[9]

Under Gavin's leadership, ADL established a Management Education Institute which by 1978 had some four hundred graduates around the world. The idea for the institute came to Gavin in 1963 in Nigeria, where he had gone to study the new nation's development program. He found that though the Nigerians received money from the United States, because they lacked management skills they could not put this aid to its best use.

After sending several staff members of ADL to Nigeria to provide management training, Gavin realized it would be more efficient to bring the Nigerians "back here where we had the total resources of ADL available, as well as the opportunity to visit American industries. From there it moved to where we are to-day."[10] Though the institute was hardly ADL's biggest money-maker, Gavin felt it was helpful in improving the lives of people in the developing nations, and in winning friends for America.

In his continuing efforts to hire minorities at ADL, Gavin's top lieutenant was Joseph Rollins. A black Chicagoan who had once worked for *Ebony,* Rollins had much experience in minority recruitment both in government and in private business. He had been an officer in a savings and loan company and had worked in many ways to support the establishment of black-owned businesses.

From Chicago he had gone to Washington in the early 1960s to join Sargent Shriver's talent search to find more black people for high-level government jobs. Later, as a special assistant to Chairman Clifford Alexander of the Equal Employment Opportunities Commission, his job was to help and encourage private industries to do the same thing. In this work Rollins and his staff called on the presidents of at least sixty major U.S. companies to tell them of the availability of black talents and resources. In the course of these calls he came to the attention of people at the Arthur D. Little Company, including ADL Board Chairman James Gavin.

At that time there were only three or four blacks on the entire ADL professional staff. All were urging that more black people be hired. In 1969 ADL offered Rollins a job in its personnel section, with the primary task of setting up an effective affirmative actions program. He accepted and came to work in Cambridge in April. Gavin soon took him aside and said, "Joe, I think we should get a black person and a female on this Board [of Directors] as soon as possible, and I mean to help."[11]

Gavin's door was always open to the candidates Rollins found. And Gavin was duly impressed with the quality of the black people who came through the door, people such as Dr. Pauli Murray, a black woman lawyer and a professor at the Boston University Law School, and John Johnson from Chicago, editor of *Ebony*. Johnson became a member of the board, as did Dr. Alonzo Yerby, a renowned black expert in community and world health programs and a member of the Harvard University Medical School.

Through the early 1970s the number of ADL black professionals—engineers, technologists, economists— expanded rapidly. At least three black women were hired. By 1979, however, the number had declined. One reason those blacks who left ADL were not replaced with other blacks seems to have been that the affirmative action program gradually lost its original energy and aggressiveness. Rollins himself moved to the marketing staff where his skills could be used on a broader front. And Gavin was preparing for retirement. His last year as board chairman was 1976.

Increasingly during his years at ADL, Gavin turned his restless mind to the social and economic problems of America and the world. In one annual report he expressed deep concern that the world was "outstripping our earthbound raw materials and resources." To solve this global problem he predicted that "all of man's institutions will have to change; his government, the infrastructure of his country, most industries, and many of his ways of doing business."[12] The 1976 annual report included the company's prediction that "by the end of the first decade of the 21st Century we could have 60 solar power stations in operation. No longer would the people and the industry of America be dependent upon any foreign source for power."[13]

During the same busy years of the ADL expansion

program, Gavin's services were also in demand on college campuses as a visiting lecturer, before Congressional committees who wanted his opinions on such matters as the North Atlantic Treaty Organization, at Tufts University where he was chairman of the Board of Visitors of the Fletcher School of Law and Diplomacy, and at a seemingly endless list of organizations ranging from the Atlantic Congress and the Atlantic Union Committee to the American Rocket Society.

In March 1964, from the University of California, he wrote to his eldest daughter Barbara:

> Lots of hard work, but extremely interesting. Most of my work has been with graduate students, dividing my time between the School of Business Administration and the Department of Political Science. . . . The campus is quite crowded, 27,500 students. But they are a much harder working group than we were in my days in college, better informed too.
>
> I started to prepare two papers to give as lectures and Cornelius Ryan convinced me that I should develop them into a small book. . . .[14]

The book was *Crisis Now,* which was published in 1968. When it appeared, Gavin was back on the nation's front pages, involved in the American tragedy called Vietnam.

X. *Good Army—Wrong War*

Probably no American military misadventure wounded Gavin more deeply than the Vietnam War. Korea had been bad enough, but at least it had had a rationale: a clear-cut case of aggression and a United Nations obligation to respond. The American failure there was due to lack of preparation, badly trained troops, and inadequate equipment.

Vietnam was especially troubling to Gavin because the American army then was the kind of army he had long wanted it to be, complete with Sky Cavalry forces. In January 1966, at the height of the conflict, he had written:

> When I retired in 1958, I said that I would be happy to serve as a private in the army if it was the kind of Army that I wanted it to be. I think it is that kind of an Army now, and I would be glad to serve in it in any grade in Vietnam or

anywhere else. It is doing a splendid job in
Vietnam and deserves the support of all our
people.[1]

Yet in the end this army was defeated by a mass of
supposedly ill-equipped peasant guerrillas. According
to Gavin, the war was lost not on the battlefield, but in
Washington. The first mistake was America's entry
into the war. Gavin was among the first to warn against
this course.

As early as May 1954, only a few days after the final
French defeat at Dien Bien Phu by the Communist
forces of Ho Chi Minh, Gavin and his immediate superi-
or, Army Chief of Staff Matthew Ridgway, made a
detailed tactical study of the situation in Southeast
Asia. Gavin fully concurred with a Ridgway "memorandum of record" pointing out the "difficulties which
would be encountered by a large, modern military force
operating in Indo-China." The memorandum observed:

> The adverse conditions prevalent in this area
> combine all those which confronted the U.S.
> forces in previous campaigns in the South and
> Southwest Pacific and Eastern Asia, with the
> additional grave complications of a large na-
> tive population, in thousands of villages, most
> of which are about evenly divided between
> friendly and hostile.
>
> The complex nature of these problems would
> require a major U.S. logistical effort. They ex-
> plode the myth that the air and sea forces could
> solve the Indo-China problems. If U.S. shore-
> based forces are projected any appreciable dis-
> tance inland, as would be essential, they will
> require constant local security at their every
> location, and for their every activity. The Army

will have to provide these forces and their total
will be very large.[2]

With the concurrence of Army Secretary Stevens, Ridgway presented these views to President Eisenhower.
Eisenhower listened quietly without comment, then
said simply, "Thank you, Matt, for coming over."[3]
Eisenhower was, of course, strongly committed to "containing" the Communists. Despite his coolness to Ridgway's visit (the two men had other differences),
Eisenhower heeded his advice. Probably he already
agreed with it before Ridgway came to his office.

Malcom Moos, a political scientist who served on
Eisenhower's White House staff during the president's
second term and later became president of the University of Minnesota, often heard Eisenhower express res-
ervations about large-scale U.S. military involvement
in Southeast Asia. On several occasions the president
said that U.S. involvement in ground troop warfare in
the area would be "a nightmarish undertaking." Moos
remembered that Eisenhower "stressed many times to
me personally about opposing his Joint Chiefs of Staff
and the French government in 1954 when an urgent
request was made for a billion dollars and 50,000 American paratroopers."[4]

Eisenhower approached Vietnam cautiously, in October 1954 offering economic aid to South Vietnam and in
early 1955 agreeing to send a handful of military advisors to help train the South Vietnamese Army. At first
only 165 went, a reasonably small commitment. During
the following six years of Eisenhower's administration,
there were never more than 2,000 Americans in South
Vietnam.

Gavin's involvement in Vietnam began while he was
ambassador to France. In the early summer of 1961,
John F. Kennedy made his first, and only, presidential

visit to Europe. Thanks in part to Gavin's preparation, Kennedy's meeting with President Charles de Gaulle was cordial. The subject of Vietnam came up only briefly, Kennedy telling de Gaulle that the U.S. had a serious problem in Vietnam, but would continue to help the Diem regime bring stability to that country. At this point, de Gaulle shrugged, spread both arms, opened his hands upward on the table, and in effect, said, "We have had all we want of Southeast Asia and we will have no more of it."[5]

From Paris Kennedy proceeded to Vienna for a very different meeting with Soviet Premier Nikita Khrushchev. Arrogant and bullying, Khrushchev threatened to take over Berlin. Kennedy later commented that the session was the "roughest thing in my life," and said, "now we have a problem of trying to make our power credible."[6]

When the president returned to Washington, he began a study of the U.S. military budget. On 31 July he announced plans for a $3.4 billion increase in the arms budget and a call-up of nearly a quarter of a million troops, including an additional combat division for Europe and additional air support. At first there was a wave of diplomatic anxiety about what Kennedy intended to do in Europe. In Paris Gavin received worried calls from other ambassadors wanting to know if Kennedy planned to go to war over Berlin. Gavin reinforced Kennedy's show of strength by telling them that the president felt if war were to come over Berlin eventually, it might as well happen sooner rather than later.

Kennedy worked for a political solution to the problems in Europe. He proposed new meetings with the Soviets, and called on foreign ambassadors in Washington to help prepare an agenda. But the new militant stance also affected Southeast Asia, where the Communists were threatening to take over Vietnam and Laos.

As Kennedy investigated the situation in Southeast Asia, he decided he needed more than routine reports from the military mission there. In the late summer of 1961 he decided to send a special observer to get more details on what was actually happening. The observer was Walt Rostow, a professor of economics from the Masachusetts Institute of Technology, whom Gavin had first met in Cambridge when they were both members of a group of advisors to Kennedy, then senator from Massachusetts. At that time Rostow seemed to have little direct interest in military operations. But soon after President Kennedy brought Rostow to Washington, the professor had asked Gavin to come to the White House to talk about insurgency and counterinsurgency.

As Rostow's trip to Vietnam drew closer, some on the White House staff worried about his increasing militancy. Several urged that someone from the State Department accompany him to provide a more diplomatic view. Secretary of State Rusk opposed this, seeing Vietnam as primarily a military rather than a political problem. Instead of a diplomat, Rostow's partner on the trip was Gen. Maxwell Taylor, Kennedy's military advisor. Gavin viewed the mission as "the beginning of the takeover of the Southeast Asian problem by the Department of Defense, and this view of the situation as primarily a defense problem and not a political one ultimately had disastrous consequences."[7]

When Taylor returned from Vietnam he prepared a report for the president urging more U.S. troops for that area, saying the advantages of increasing American strength in Vietnam outweighed the disadvantages. He recommended sending in at least eight thousand more men if necessary. Though he admitted there was a possibility of getting into a major war, he felt the chance was slight. He observed that North Vietnam was ex-

tremely vulnerable to conventional bombing, a weak-
ness which should be exploited diplomatically.

Kennedy was surprised, if not shocked, that the army
seemed to be reversing its position of "no more Koreas."
But on 1 October 1962, less than a year after his hawkish
report, Taylor was made chairman of the joint chiefs of
staff. Under President Lyndon Johnson, he would become U.S. ambassador to Saigon.

Meanwhile, under the auspices of Communist North
Vietnam, the National Liberation Front (Vietcong) had
gained strength in South Vietnam. Terrorism increased, especially in the villages as the Vietcong
sought power through kidnappings and murders of officials. Kennedy sent in more U.S. forces. It is true that at
the time of his death the Americans in Vietnam were
still considered military advisors, an adjunct to the
South Vietnamese army which was supposed to be
fighting its own war. It is also true that from a peak of
sixteen thousand during the Kennedy years, the number of Americans in Vietnam had actually been reduced
slightly by the time of the assassination.

Yet, as Gavin noted later, the aid from both
Eisenhower and Kennedy, which was intended to help
the South Vietnamese army stand on its own feet, actually made the South Vietnamese more dependent on
Washington, less eager to do what was needed to build
up their own defenses. Add to this the corruption and
inefficiency of the Saigon government, and the prospects were not bright for a strong and independent
South Vietnam. Gavin believed that "President
Eisenhower and his administration left office without
ever really understanding the extent to which this nation was committed to South Vietnam." Although ini-
tially there were only a few hundred U.S. advisors there,
"those men had made a tremendous impact upon the
thinking and actions of the South Vietnamese military

minds who felt they could look up to the Great White
Father in Washington for help."[8]

When, in late 1963, Lyndon Johnson succeeded the
assassinated John Kennedy in the White House, Gavin
was an active Democrat, a member of the Massachusetts Democratic Advisory Council. He voted for Johnson
in 1964, like many other Americans of both parties who
feared the militant posture of Johnson's opponent, Sen.
Barry Goldwater of Arizona. But in 1967 Gavin not only
refused to support Johnson, but himself became a potential Independent nominee for president.

The series of events that led to this split began even
before the 1964 election, in a place of which most Americans were then only dimly aware—the Gulf of Tonkin
off the coast of North Vietnam. On 2 August 1964 two
U.S. destroyers, the *Maddox* and the *C. Turner Joy,*
were reportedly attacked in the gulf by North Vietnamese torpedo boats. Five days later, at Johnson's
urging, Congress passed the fateful Gulf of Tonkin
Resolution, giving the president power to "take all necessary measures to repel any armed attack against the
Armed Forces of the United States and to prevent further aggression."[9] Few resisted Johnson's political
moves to obtain this authority. Gavin would later ask:
"Suppose Russia had provoked the same incident.
Would [Johnson] have received such tremendous support to act against Russia? Hell, no!"[10]

Newly inaugurated as president for another four
years and armed with the Gulf of Tonkin Resolution,
Johnson quickly moved into the hawkish position that
his supporters had feared Goldwater would take. By
February 1965, he had ordered continuous bombing
raids over North Vietnam below the twentieth parallel.
By mid-1965 American commanders were authorized to
commit 23,000 of the "advisors" to combat in South
Vietnam. By the end of the year U.S. army, navy, and

marine forces in action in South Vietnam numbered some 184,000. Within another year there were more than 385,000 U.S. troops there, and another 60,000 in the fleet and some 33,000 in Thailand.

Gavin saw nothing but disaster ahead. But he knew that for political reasons Johnson could not simply withdraw from Vietnam on short notice. Johnson remembered that a Democratic administration had been accused of "losing" China to the Communists, and he had said he did not intend to be "the first American President to lose a war."[11] Instead of a precipitous retreat, Gavin proposed an "Enclave Theory." He explained his plan in a long letter to *Harper's* which was published in the February issue, but as early as 16 January excerpts from the letter appeared in many newspapers.

Gavin said the war effort in Vietnam was "too costly and too risky." While he was disturbed by "moral aspects" of the war, he intended to discuss only tactical and strategic problems. He proposed a permanent end to the bombing of North Vietnam and a decision to limit U.S. military operations to holding "coastal enclaves" in South Vietnam while working for a political solution in the United Nations or at Geneva. The enclaves he suggested were

> Camranh Bay, Danang, and similar areas where American bases are being established. However, we are stretching these resources beyond reason in our endeavors to secure the entire country of South Vietnam from the Vietcong penetration. This situation, of course, is caused by the growing Vietcong strength ... we simply have to make up our mind what we want to do and then provide the resources necessary to do it. If our objective is to secure all of South

Vietnam, then forces should be deployed on the
17th parallel and along the Cambodian border
adequate to do this. In view of the nature of the
terrain, it might be necessary to extend our
defenses on the 17th parallel to the Mekong
River and across part of Thailand. Such a
course would take many times as much force as
we now have in Vietnam.

To increase the bombing and to bomb
Hanoi—or even Peking—will add to our problems rather than detract from them, and it will
not stop the penetrations of North Vietnam
troops into the south. Also if we were to quadru-
ple, for example, our combat forces there, we
should then anticipate the intervention of Chinese "volunteers" and the reopening of the
Korean front. This seems to be the ultimate
prospect of the course that we are now on.

On the other hand, if we should maintain
enclaves on the coast, desist in our bombing
attacks in North Vietnam, and seek to find a
solution through the United Nations or a conference in Geneva, we could very likely do so
with the forces now available . . . the problems
that we would then have to deal with would be
far less than those associated with the expansion of the conflict.[12]

Many Americans then belived that the Vietcong
posed a threat to U.S. interests throughout the Pacific
and because of the "Domino Theory" that if North
Vietnam defeated South Vietnam, the Communists
would eventually invade Hawaii. Gavin, "the first well-
known military professional to dispute" this theory,[13]
wrote:

I do not for a moment think that if we should withdraw from Vietnam the next stop would be Waikiki. The Kra Peninsula, Thailand, and the Philippines can all be secured, although we ultimately might have heavy fighting on the northern frontiers of Thailand. But we should be realistic about the dangers of the course we are now on. . . . To get to the heart of the problem, I doubt that world opinion would tolerate the bombing and seizure of Manchuria. If the Chinese Communists continue on their present course of aggression and, at the same time, continue to develop more devastating weapons—and I refer to nuclear weapons—the time may come when China will bring upon herself a nuclear war. . . . In the meantime, we must do the best we can with the forces we have deployed to Vietnam, keeping in mind the true meaning of strategy in global affairs. . . . Since the advent of the Space Age, there has been a revolution in the nature of war and global conflict. The confrontation in Vietnam is the first test of our understanding of such change, or our lack of it. The measures that we must now take in Southeast Asia must stem from sagacity and thoughtfulness, and an awareness of the nature of strategy in this rapidly shrinking world.[14]

On 4 February Gen. Maxwell Taylor publicly repudiated the enclave idea. While not mentioning Gavin by name, Taylor said such an action would amount to a "crushing defeat of international proportions" for America and a victory for Hanoi and Peking. He said the U.S. could not run away from "its destiny as the champion of the free world," and he told reporters he knew of no active senior officer involved in Vietnam policy decisions who agreed with the proposals in Gavin's letter.[15]

Gavin had proposed the enclave theory to start some debate on the merits. He knew from personal observation and experience that all was not as it should be in a particular area about which he had knowledge, and he wanted to do what he could to remedy the situation.

Among many who opposed the enclave theory in 1965 was Defense Secretary Robert McNamara. Despite his opposition, however, McNamara invited Gavin to Washington to talk things over. The defense secretary pointed out that Gavin's enclaves would be under enemy artillery and mortar fire. Gavin agreed that at times they could be, but argued that if the defense forces around them were highly mobile they could be held long enough to assure a withdrawal. McNamara

> did not seem satisfied with my answer, so I suggested to him that the alternative was going to be a disaster sooner or later, with many more lives lost. He said he didn't want to think about that, he wanted to think about how to make the present situation work. . . . I felt genuinely sorry for him for he was a very dedicated man doing his best under extremely difficult circumstances. . . . As I left his office, I remember turning at the door and saying to him, "I wouldn't be in your shoes for anything."[16]

Gavin felt that McNamara was being misled by faulty intelligence estimates and optimistic reports. In the State Department there were some outspoken skeptics such as George Ball, but McNamara had no dissenters in the Defense Department. He relied mostly on reports from Saigon, which gave scaled-down figures because, as a general in William Westmoreland's office reportedly said, "Jesus, if we tell this to the people in Washington we'll be out of the war tomorrow."[17]

Would Gavin's enclave plan have worked? Even with years of hindsight and a consensus that the alternative course was, indeed, the disaster Gavin foresaw, there is still disagreement about his proposal. Lt. Gen. Richard Seitz, one of Gavin's close comrades during the early airborne days, said that, "when the President committed the United States to military action in Vietnam, he should have at the same time made a clear and unequivocal commitment to employ the full U.S. military capability to bring the war to an early and successful conclusion."[18]

Gen. Anthony McAuliffe of Bastogne fame, however, agreed with Gavin and felt his theory was "much sounder than the procedure we followed." He observed that Taylor eventually "pretty much adopted Gavin's Enclave Theory."[19] Westmoreland also turned to the idea several years after Gavin proposed it. Gavin said:

> I had a most interesting experience. I was in General Westmoreland's office where he has a three by four black board with an outline of Vietnam in white paint with the river and Saigon shown on it, and in the course of this discussion about the strength of his position there he got up with a piece of chalk, drew a circle around Danang, Camranh Bay, and Saigon, pointing out these enclaves gave him a real base of power. This is exactly what I maintained in '65.[20]

Columnist Walter Lippmann called Gavin's plan "the best of a bad business, not glorious but the least costly way of repairing the grievous mistakes of the past."[21]

But Gen. J. Lawton Collins, former army chief of staff, chairman of the joint chiefs, and onetime U.S. ambassador to NATO, disagreed. Gavin had been wrong, Collins felt,

> when he got out of the Army. He stated that he could do more for the Army outside than in. I thoroughly disagree. And I think it has worked out that way. . . . Let me also say that I think he was a great soldier. I think he did a wonderful job as a paratrooper, and I had nothing but admiration for his ability to lead men in action. . . . Now with respect to his enclave theory, again I thoroughly disagree. . . . Had we withdrawn into a series of enclaves . . . what would happen? We would have been turning the country over to the Communists and we would be nesting inside an enclave, doing what? I don't know. It would have permitted the Communists, in my opinion, to just take over the rest of the country and they would have paid no attention to us and just would have let us stay in our enclave . . . prior to Dien Bien Phu . . . I saw in Hanoi in the Red River Delta area, which is the heart of North Vietnam, what the French had by this stage. What had happened was the French had gradually lost control of the outer provinces, that is the countryside, and they had withdrawn into a series of enclaves, actually they were fortified positions, but not continuous.
>
> The Communists were roaming the countryside. And I was impressed at the time that the French were going to get nowhere under any such system as that. They were going to lose the Red River Delta because they had given

up the countryside. And all they had done was to go into a series of set defenses, which never has worked anywhere in military history that I know of.

It seems to me that Gavin's proposition of having our forces withdraw into a series of enclaves along the coastline in South Vietnam was quite comparable to what the French had done and I had seen failing with my own eyes. And I knew from my study of military history it wasn't going to work. I don't think [Gavin's] enclave system would have worked either.

General Collins was considerably more supportive of Gavin's position that we should never have put ground combat troops into Vietnam in the first place:

In my judgment, two big mistakes were made in our handling of the Vietnamese situation. First of all was the decision to put American Army troops on the ground in Vietnam. . . . The question of putting Army troops on the ground never arose during the time I was down there. If it had arisen, I would have opposed it. . . . The second mistake was that, in having decided to put some troops in on the ground, we should have gone all out then. If we were going to do it at all, then was the time to do it, rather than to do it piecemeal.[22]

Despite the comparisons with Dien Bien Phu, there was a vast difference between the French tactics and Gavin's plan for South Vietnam. The French tried to use enclaves as a means to subdue, conquer, and control the territory militarily. Gavin's enclaves would have been strong points, mostly on the coast, from which to move out, patrol the periphery, solicit help wherever possible, then return to the enclave, which could be secured against attacks through use of new weaponry and systems.

Dien Bien Phu was an inland enclave on an exposed plain with no escape except by air. When it was encircled, the only way to reinforce it was to drop parachutists and supplies. Gavin's concept never envisioned such a vulnerable position. In his plan, evacuation could have been by helicopter or boat from a shoreline under complete control of American forces.

A more important question, perhaps, is how receptive the Communists would have been to ideas for a political solution while the United States held enclaves in South Vietnam. In his testimony before the Senate Armed Services Committee in January 1966, Gen. Earle G. Wheeler, chairman of the joint chiefs of staff, argued that if the U.S. stopped bombing and withdrew to enclaves "there would be very little point in negotiation ... there would be no pressure on the North Vietnamese to negotiate under such circumstances, so why should they negotiate?"[23] Gavin believed the North Vietnamese would feel pressured to get the American troops out of Vietnam, and would negotiate for that reason.

Despite the rejection of his enclave plan, Gavin continued his fight against the U.S. military escalation in Vietnam through 1966 and 1967. Much of his effort came in testimony before Congressional committees. On 9 February 1966 he told the Senate Foreign Relations Committee that, in his opinion, a significant increase in the number of American troops in Vietnam would involve the risk of war with China. At the same time, such escalation would erode our ability to meet commitments in other parts of the world.

He told the senators that he felt the government had become so "mesmerized" by Vietnam that its commitments there had become "alarmingly out of balance." As for the bombing of North Vietnam, Gavin said it would achieve little, and warned of a bad impact on world public opinion—especially if civilian centers near target areas were hit.[24]

Nevertheless, the escalation continued. By early 1967 there was even heavier bombing of the North. The administration's position seemed to be that the bombing would force Hanoi to the peace table, and Johnson indicated the bombing would stop as soon as Hanoi agreed to negotiate. Actually, the bombs only stiffened the North's resistance. On 21 February 1967 Gavin was again invited to appear before the senate committee. He urged an immediate and unconditional halt of American bombing (except for tactical use), as a first step toward a political settlement of the war.

Gavin called the bombing of targets near populated areas "militarily as well as morally wrong." They had, he said, caused many civilian casualties, had failed to stop the flow of supplies to the South, and had aroused "the ill will of people around the world."[25]

But the bombing went on, the ground escalation continued, and by the end of 1967, the number of U.S. troops in Vietnam reached nearly 475,000. Protests, especially among the young, increased. On 21 and 22 October there were massive antiwar rallies in Washington. Some demonstrators tried to storm the Pentagon, and hundreds were arrested.

At the same time, black unrest was growing, especially in big city ghettoes where poverty and frustration were erupting into angry riots. Gavin reflected bitterly that while American cities decayed, the government was spending an estimated $25,000 per man to kill enemy soldiers in Vietnam.

In addition to the moral issues of the war and its effect on American commitments in other parts of the world,

Gavin perceived tactical errors in the military operations themselves. At first the Americans had failed to
learn from the experiences of the French, who Gavin
believed had lost because they could not use their mechanized forces against an enemy who was not bound by
roads. The few roads available were always under
enemy observation, were easily mined, and well suited
for ambush. Well-equipped U.S. troops, organized into
division-sized units, highly mechanized, and trained in
concepts applicable to a European war, were sent to
South Vietnam only to be ambushed repeatedly. Gavin
recalled his unheeded warnings of the early 1950s that
the United States should be prepared for *any* kind of
war.[26]

Years later Gen. Matthew Ridgway said that the
Vietnam venture was doomed from the start because "it
was a war we could not win." He believed Americans
had been "trying to kill an idea with bomb and bullet,
which cannot be done except by genocide and the oblit-
eration of nuclear attack (which would have been anything but a 'win') in a country where at least half the
population was hostile, and the people indifferent as to
who governed in Saigon because their lot was always
the same. It was the most egregious mistake any U.S.
Government has ever made."[27]

If there was any comfort at all for Gavin in Vietnam,
it was that his Sky Cavalry concept finally came into
use. Troop-carrying helicopters and helicopter gun-
ships became a common sight in Southeast Asia, giving
U.S. forces the mobility they could never have achieved
on the ground. Even with Sky Cavalry, however, the
jungle trails, the faulty intelligence, and the divided
allegiance of the people themselves presented formidable obstacles. Asked in an interview in Cambridge in
1978 why Sky Cavalry was unable to win the war, Gavin
said, "Well, let me put it this way. We would have done a
hell of a lot worse without it."[28]

Increasingly, Gavin saw the roots of the Vietnam problem in Washington itself. "Somebody asked me whether our biggest problems are in Vietnam or here," he said.

> I had to answer here. Now, that's a hell of a thing to have to admit, but it's true; the riots, poor housing, so many things half done. And it's the war that has allowed this to grow. . . . The troops are doing what they have to do, and doing it well. The things that are done wrong, the wrong decisions, are done here."[29]

By late summer of 1967, Gavin decided to take his ideas more directly into the political arena. In August he resigned from the sixteen-man Massachusetts Democratic Advisory Council. He gave his own business pressures as one reason, but when questioned further by reporters he replied with his usual candor that he "simply will not support Johnson for reelection in 1968. And obviously anyone on the Council should be ready to do so."[30]

In an article on the resignation, the *Boston Globe* said Gavin's action was a "much clearer statement of what he believes American objectives should be: de-escalation, negotiation and withdrawal from Vietnam, even if this means Communist influence (or domination) in a new Vietnamese government. . . . Like many others, Gavin seems to have despaired of the relatively friendly pressure that senate testimony and magazine articles can bring on President Johnson. He is determined to play a part in defeating Johnson for re-election next year."[31]

In late 1967, at the invitation of Gen. William Westmoreland, Gavin visited Vietnam. The trip reinforced his belief that, as he said in Vietnam at "a dinner table conversation ... the U.S. should never have gotten into the war in the first place."[32]

While a few people at ADL were concerned about their chief executive officer being viewed as a controversial figure, most staff members knew Gavin spoke with military knowledge and insight and respected his views. Cyril Herrmann believed "most of the staff at ADL were proud of General Gavin for being the first to challenge (openly) the conduct of the war in Vietnam. We were able to take it in stride when he was criticised. ... By this time, of course, General Gavin was firmly established with ADL, and he had as high a percentage of supporters within our company as he must have had when he was commanding the 82nd Airborne."[33]

In September 1967 Gavin began conferring with prominent Republicans such as former Gov. William Scranton of Pennsylvania and Sen. Thruston Morton of Kentucky. His goal was to have the Republican national convention in 1968 oppose Johnson's war policies, and nominate a candidate who would follow through on this opposition.

The presidential election year of 1968 was a chaotic one for America. Angry blacks rioted from Washington, D.C., to the Watts area of Los Angeles. On 4 April in Memphis, Tennessee, the black leader who had urged a peaceful path to racial justice—Dr. Martin Luther King, Jr.—was assassinated. More rioting followed, and Chicago's Mayor Richard Daley issued "shoot to kill" orders against arsonists. At the Democratic national convention in August, Chicago became the scene of more violence with over ten thousand young war protesters, mostly white, battling with the police.

Americans were looking for new leadership in the White House, someone who could steer the nation to a peaceful solution of both international and domestic strife. Since Gavin's break with Johnson and the Massachusetts Democratic advisory group in 1967, increasing numbers of Americans thought he might be the man they sought. He received hundreds of letters urging him to declare himself a candidate for the presidency. Gavin felt that only a Republican president could free America from its involvement in Vietnam. The idea "that he himself could be a candidate sounds as fantastic to him as it does to any objective observer of the confused political scene. But it is no more fantastic than his own career."[34]

While much of the mail envisioned Gavin as a Republican candidate because of his break with the Massachusetts Democratic Council, Allard K. Lowenstein, former vice-president of the Americans for Democratic Action and a friend of Sen. Robert Kennedy, approached him with the suggestion that he run for the Democratic nomination. Lowenstein had first tried to get Robert Kennedy to run, then Congressman Don Edwards of California, and John Kenneth Galbraith, the economist and former ambassador to India. When all had turned him down, Lowenstein went to see Gavin in Boston. Gavin was "most pleasant and sympathetic and even willing to be a candidate, but not a Democratic candidate. 'Do you see yourself getting the Republican nomination?' said Lowenstein in horror."[35]

Among others who tried to promote Gavin's candidacy was an antiwar group in Lexington, Massachusetts, called the "Citizens to Draft Gavin," which financed a newspaper advertising campaign. But Gavin later said of his supporters, "I guess they just ran out of gas."[36]

Had Sen. George McGovern, whom Lowenstein approached after Gavin in 1968, been elected president in 1972, Gavin might have become U.S. secretary of defense. In 1975 McGovern said:

Had we been successful in 1972, it is very likely
that I would have asked General Gavin to head
the Department of Defense. I have been particularly impressed over the years with his ability to measure national security in more than
military terms, a concept which has always
been of major concern to me. His military in-
sights on Vietnam were invaluable . . . I felt
General Gavin would be uniquely well-
qualified to translate policy changes into action.[37]

But in 1968 the Democrats nominated Vice-President
Hubert H. Humphrey, who was identified with Johnson
policies. The Republican candidate was Richard M.
Nixon, a man with impeccable anti-Communist credentials, but also one who said he had a plan to end the war.
After Nixon's election the Paris peace talks were expanded to include the Vietcong as well as North and
South Vietnam. By summer, Nixon began a gradual
withdrawal of American ground combat troops and the
assumption of primary combat responsibilities by the
South Vietnamese themselves. In July the first U.S.
troops were pulled out. But the big bombers remained in
Vietnam, and domestic protest continued.

On 18 December, as the peace talks faltered, Nixon
ordered the heaviest bombing of the war against North
Vietnam. Finally, on 8 January 1973, the talks resumed
and Nixon ordered a halt to all U.S. offensive military
operations in Vietnam. Soon the North Vietnamese
were on the attack again. After some resistance, the
army of the South was in retreat, then in a rout. By the
end of April 1975, Saigon surrendered to Hanoi.

Everything the United States had gone into Vietnam
to save was now lost. "Vietnamization" had not been
enough, yet in 1969 Nixon knew that the word would

sound good to Americans who felt they had done enough. Possibly it was the only politically feasible way out. But, to the extent that the administration knew the South Vietnamese could not survive, the plan was at least tainted with political press-agentry. To that extent, the United States got out of the war the same way it got in—through deceit of the American people.

The cost of the U.S. involvement was more than forty-six thousand American combat deaths, an estimated total death toll of two million, a scarred Southeast Asian landscape that would take decades to rebuild, and billions of wasted dollars that could have been used to improve American cities and American society. Gavin predicted there would be "a tendency to sweep all of this under the rug."[38] He took no comfort in having foreseen the Vietnam tragedy, but at the same time he hoped it would not be forgotten that he had fought so hard to avoid it.

The anger and confusion of the Vietnam years had produced some strange and painful incidents for Gavin. One event occurred when he and Jean were walking to the auditorium of Boston College for the graduation of Aileen, his second daughter. A woman lashed out at Gavin, calling him a warmonger. Cut by this harsh and unexpected public insult, Gavin asked what she meant. She accused him of supporting the war in Vietnam and even of becoming a participant in making it the policy to harm our country. When Gavin had a chance to speak, he informed her that she was mistaken and that he had spent a considerable part of his life in fighting against involvement in the Vietnam War. He then asked her if she knew who he was, and she said yes, "you're Maxwell Taylor."

XI. *The View from Acorn Park*

Gavin had been proven right about Sky Cavalry, the single-option massive retaliation policy, and the superiority of limited wars over "total victories." He was happy that the B-1 bomber program was halted. But he had still other ideas he wanted to see adopted. Listing in one column on a green chalkboard "military" and "hardware" and in another economic policies, diplomacy, social development, education, and health, he drew a line between the two columns and insisted:

these must be brought together. The military men must understand this and stop relying on military hardware as our only defense tool.

Look at Japan. It spends only $8 billion on its military forces and is challenging this nation and the world in many economic fields. In 1978 we'll spend about $136 billion plus to try to catch up with the Russian weapons advances.

... The stupidity is obvious if we fail to realize that it will be the balance of economic power and trade that will bring stability.[1]

The components of a rational defense program must include the rebuilding of America's decaying cities, the development of new energy sources, racial understanding, more educational and employment opportunities, improved health care, and so forth. Summing up, Gavin observed that in Vietnam Americans fought "for the Communists." The Russian and Chinese were happy to see the United States pin down over half a million troops and lose billions of dollars worth of military equipment in that part of the world. While Americans must be stationed in Western Europe for defense purposes, it is highly doubtful the Soviet Union intends to invade the area. The United States must not overcommit itself in Europe and neglect to strengthen its position in the East, where a head-on clash with the U.S.S.R. might occur.[2]

Still clearly concerned about radiation, Gavin said the neutron bomb could pose serious dangers for friend and foe alike. The concern for more civilian and less Pentagon control of American policy seems to have dominated much of Gavin's thinking for more than a decade. In early 1977, he had been prominently mentioned as a leading candidate for chief of the much maligned Central Intelligence Agency, though he was not eager for the job. He still believed the State Department should be America's first line of defense, but thought it understaffed and undertrained compared with the Pentagon. Military training should be improved, too, with ethics a required subject at West Point. To Gavin, an ethical outlook should be an integral part of a soldier's character.[3]

When the CIA appointment went instead to Adm.

Stansfield Turner, Gavin called it a "good choice," but
added: "In a way I regretted to see a man in uniform
taking [the CIA] over. The intelligence estimates of the
CIA are, all too often, the basis for a budget request in
the Pentagon. It is an unhealthy situation. Civilianiza-
tion is what is needed in the CIA at this time."[4]

Gavin had believed for years that the Strategic Air
Command, with its limited nuclear capability, was no
longer a valid instrument in the American arsenal, and
that a crash program was needed to bring about a more
sophisticated space-age military structure. As far back
as 1957 Gavin and Von Braun had talked about anti-
satellite missiles propelled by solar energy.

When asked about his retirement from the army,
Gavin replied without hesitation, "Some may say this is
the greatest mistake I ever made in my life. But if I had
to I would do it all over again." He paused briefly,
smiled, and added, "I might, however, engage the services of a good public relations man."[5]

Thanks in part to Lyndon Johnson's out-of-context
notes to the press from a supposedly closed senate
hearing room, many people believed Gavin retired early
simply because he was frustrated and angry that he
was not given a fourth star. But Gavin was "never
disenchanted with the Army or with the service." He
had been

> disenchanted with the way of the Administra-
> tion and some of the Joint Chiefs of Staff were
> thinking and operating. And it's difficult to live
> with a system which has inherent in it the
> mentalities that we faced regarding massive
> retaliation and the view that the world was
> divided into good guys and bad guys. . . no
> effort [was] made for reconciliation or accep-
> tance of constructive criticism of those things

which were wrong. And, mark my words, just as the errors of the past have been thrown into our faces today, we're going to see the errors of today thrown into the faces of our children.[6]

Americans may again be "faced with. . .a two-front war unless we change our thinking and begin to recognize that we are part of the world and that it is no longer subservient to the dictates of those in Washington."[7]

Certainly Gavin's impatience with things as they are helped put him on his collision course with the Washington brass. But Air Force Gen. Carl Spaatz obviously shared Gavin's own belief in candor when he wrote:

Was Gavin being insubordinate when he said the Joint Chiefs of Staff should be reorganized under a single Chief of Staff to give the President better advice than he is now getting? Or was his first obligation to be honest with himself and with Congress?

Clearly, Gavin had no honorable choice but to express his own best opinion when asked for it. . . . The present Joint Chiefs of Staff setup is not sacrosanct. And it has become so major a part of the defense picture that the pros and cons of change should be debated openly and frankly, not only by Congress but by the public as well. . . . In the predicament in which the country finds itself, it will do well to listen to such officers as Gavin on questions of military organization. . . .[8]

Some have compared Gavin's clash with administration policies with that of Gen. Douglas MacArthur during the Korean War. But there are vast differences. MacArthur's attack on the Truman administration reached far beyond the limits of military responsibility and into the sphere of domestic politics. MacArthur's greatest mistake was to respond to Rep. Joseph Martin, Jr., then Republican leader in the House of Representatives, in a political appeal clearly designed to provide ammunition against the president's policies. In effect, he openly aligned himself with the Republican opposition to Truman.

Gavin, too, opposed administration policies. But he made no such partisan appeals. True, he was used for political purposes, but his own intent was never to exploit political divisiveness. Rather, in a quiet and unassuming way, unlike MacArthur's pomposity, he was seeking a consensus.

Others have tried to draw a parallel between Gavin and Gen. Billy Mitchell, who was court-martialed for trying too hard to bring the army into the air age in the 1920s. But again, the tactics of the dissenters followed different paths. Mitchell was harsh, shrill, and public, often given to overstatement. At one point he accused the military leaders of virtual treason for failing to accept his ideas about air power. In contrast, Gavin's arguments were calm, reasoned, and usually given as answers to Congressional questions in what he had presumed were closed hearings.

Most importantly, Gavin came to see the military forces as only one part of the complex machinery needed to preserve peace, or at least to limit the scope of war. Mitchell was talking only about a new weapon and MacArthur only about a strategy for military triumph. While Gavin worked for a better and stronger army, he knew that political solutions, especially in the nuclear age, were necessary. The broad range of his concerns was demonstrated in June 1977.

In Boston on 13 June, Gavin was an honored guest at the premiere of *A Bridge Too Far,* the film version of

Cornelius Ryan's book about the battle of the Holland
Bridges in World War II. The gala day had begun with
parachute jumps in the afternoon on Boston Common.
At the evening premiere Gavin was the center of attention. As Mayor Kevin White introduced Gavin to the
audience, he asked if anyone wished to recognize the
general. Members of the Jim Gavin Chapter of the 82nd
Airborne Division, of the 101st Airborne Division Chapter, and others who had served Gavin rose to face him in
a show of silent respect.

Only three days earlier, in Gallia County, Ohio,
Gavin and his family had attended a far different ceremony, the dedication of an electric power plant which
bore his name. A mural depicting the 82nd Airborne
Division, done by Lindsay Prescott, a longtime friend of
Gavin, was unveiled. But it was more than Gavin's
wartime exploits that brought the Ohio Power Company to name the plant for him. The young commander
had become a veteran director of the American Electric
Power Company, and was deeply concerned with the
problems of energy both in America and in the world.

Still, energy was only one issue of importance to
Gavin. In an address in Chicago in 1968, in the wake of
urban riots, he had said:

> To transform our decaying American environ-
> ment will be long and difficult. In comparison
> with our domestic crisis, Vietnam is simple.
> Since I am urging that we as a nation take far-
> reaching action to solve this crisis, I think it
> important to say what I believe.
>   I believe in excellence for all. I believe the full
> life belongs to every citizen as a birthright. I
> believe we should abolish poverty not out of
> charity but because poverty shames us as a
> nation. I believe we should totally end discrimi-

nation, not to "be nice to Negroes," but because prejudice kills the dream we could all become.

I want to abolish "we" and "they." To have both white and black become "we." The "we" of *e pluribus unum. . . .*[9]

In another speech he mentioned

our inability to understand and cope with the technological application of science to our society. . . .It is compelling that we deal with our domestic condition as a matter of highest priority. Every intellectual and physical resource that we have must be given priority response to this unprecedented challenge. It is not a case of what we may do or should do, it is what we must do.[10]

He made many of the same points in *Crisis Now,* published in 1968:

Domestically, America had begun a new revolution. I use the word "revolution" precisely and not as a figure of speech. Unless we realize the size and nature of our problem, any answer we give will be too little and too late—indeed quite irrelevant. Violence will increase and the overall breakdown of our national life will follow as a scientific certainty.[11]

Typically, he saw rational, objective thought, what one might call a scientific approach, as the way to a solution. Among other things, he proposed a group similar to the National Security Council to advise the president on urban affairs. He also called for the setting up of groups like the Manhattan Engineer District (which developed the atomic bomb) to bring the best scientific and industrial minds to bear on the growing urban crisis.

Gavin had, of course, learned from hard experience that change is not easy to implement. "It is much easier to destroy a new idea than it is to support it," he wrote in 1967, "and my experience suggests that men and their institutions are by nature conservative and resistant to change. Yet it is only through change that progress is made."[12]

Far beyond America's domestic problems, Gavin had again looked to a new technology to reduce the danger of global war, and to change many of the basic conditions that lie at the root of international conflicts. As early as 1966 he advocated a "global communications systems under an international body, the U.N., for example, that will begin to minimize the dangers of a nuclear holocaust."[13] Such a communications network could also provide the base for a true world community, reaching into every village and hamlet with information on weather, agriculture, education, and news that could help dispel much political and cultural misunderstanding among nations.

Gavin's children have scattered from New York to California. His daughter by his first marriage, the "Dear Babe" of his many wartime letters, is now Mrs. Clarence Fauntleroy and lives in Simsbury, Connecticut. Caroline, now Mrs. Richard O'Neill, works for the Department of Justice. Patricia works in Hollywood for the American Federation of Radio and TV Artists. Aileen, a graphic designer, is married to Alan C. R. Lewis. Chloe, the youngest, attends law school. Now over seventy, Gavin himself still spends many hours each week writing, painting, and golfing. His latest book, *On to Berlin,* sparked a revival of research on World War II. Though he is "not one to stop," as his daughter Aileen said,[14] Gavin realizes that others will have to continue the battles he has fought. He hopes he has set a good example.

Notes

Chapter I

[1] U.S., Congress, Senate, Subcommittee on the Air Force of the Committee on Armed Services, *Study of Airpower,* 84th Cong., 2d sess., 25 May 1956, p. 810.

[2] Ibid., p. 858.

[3] Ibid., p. 860.

[4] Ibid., p. 860–61.

[5] *New York Times,* 27 June 1956, p. 1.

[6] Ibid., 30 June 1956, p. 9.

[7] Gavin to Biggs, 29 August 1975.

[8] U.S., Department of Defense, "Memorandum for the Assistant Secretary of Defense (International Security Affairs) August 24, 1956. Subject: Gavin Testimony," Appendix.

[9] Gavin to Biggs, 29 August 1975.

[10] Biggs interview with Gavin, 20 January 1967.

Chapter II

[1] James M. Gavin, *War and Peace in the Space Age* (New York: Harper & Bros., 1956), p. 30.

[2]Ibid., p. 31.

[3]Ibid., p. 33.

[4]Ibid., p. 34.

[5]Ibid., p. 35.

[6]*New York Times,* 4 September 1939, p. 6.

[7]Gavin, *War and Peace,* p. 37.

[8]Ibid., p. 45.

[9]*New York Times,* 21 May 1941, p. 1.

[10]Gavin, *War and Peace,* p. 47.

[11]Ibid., p. 45.

[12]Biggs interview with Gavin, 18 August 1972.

[13]Quoted in Col. Barney Oldfield, "Cat Among the Chicken," *Armed Forces Journal, International,* October 1975, pp. 19–21.

[14]Biggs interview with Gavin, 28 June 1972.

[15]Ibid.

[16]Biggs interview with McAuliffe, 28 April 1973.

Chapter III

[1]James M. Gavin, *War and Peace in the Space Age* (New York: Harper & Bros., 1956), p. 53.

[2]John Thompson, "Finds No Lark—Newsman Chutes into Sicily, Decides He'll Stick to Writing," Washington *Times-Herald,* 19 July 1943, pp. 1–2.

[3]Ibid.

[4]John Thompson, "Heroism of Airborne Force Opened Way to Vittoria Area," Washington *Evening Star,* 16 July 1943, p. A-4.

[5]James M. Gavin, "Paratroopers Over Sicily," *The Infantry Journal,* November 1945, p. 25.

[6]Gavin to Barbara Gavin, undated.

[7]Thompson to Biggs, 20 January 1975.

[8]Ibid.

[9]Gavin to Barbara Gavin, 21 September 1943.

[10]James M. Gavin, "Backdoor to Normandy," *The Infantry Journal,* November 1946, p. 12.

[11]Gavin to Barbara Gavin, 6 July 1943.

[12]Gavin to Barbara Gavin, 15 July 1943.

[13]Gavin to Barbara Gavin, 26 July 1942.
[14]Gavin to Barbara Gavin, 1 August 1943.
[15]Gavin to Barbara Gavin, 21 October 1943.
[16]Gavin, "Backdoor to Normandy," p. 12.
[17]Gavin to Barbara Gavin, 2 August 1944.
[18]Gavin to Barbara Gavin, 16 August 1944.
[19]Biggs interview with Norton, 18 June 1947.
[20]Biggs interview with Collingwood, 12 February 1973.
[21]Gavin to Barbara Gavin, 16 January 1945.
[22]Gavin to Barbara Gavin, 17 April 1945.
[23]Gavin to Barbara Gavin, 21 March 1945.
[24]Thompson to Biggs, 20 January 1975.
[25]Gavin to Barbara Gavin, 11 October 1945.
[26]Gavin to Barbara Gavin, 19 September 1945.
[27]Gavin to Barbara Gavin, 30 September 1945.
[28]Anonymous to Gavin, 19 October 1945.
[29]Thompson to Biggs, 20 January 1975.
[30]Biggs interview with Gavin, 14 March 1977.
[31]*New York Times,* 13 January 1946.

Chapter IV

[1]Biggs interview with Gavin, 26 December 1967.
[2]Ibid.
[3]Ibid.
[4]James M. Gavin, *War and Peace in the Space Age* (New York: Harper & Bros., 1956), p. 107.
[5]Biggs interview with Gavin, 14 November 1976.
[6]Ibid.
[7]James M. Gavin, *Airborne Warfare* (Washington, D.C.: The Infantry Journal Press, 1947), p. 140.
[8]Gavin, *War and Peace,* p. 108.
[9]Ibid.
[10]James M. Gavin with Arthur T. Hadley, *Crisis Now* (New York: Random House, 1968), p. 25.
[11]Dwight D. Eisenhower, *At Ease* (Garden City, N.Y.: Doubleday and Company, Inc., 1967), p. 319.
[12]Biggs interview with Gavin, 9 December 1968.
[13]*Foreign Affairs,* July 1947, pp. 575 and 582.

[14]Gavin to Biggs, 31 March 1978.

[15]Biggs interview with Gavin, 14 August 1975.

[16]Gavin to Biggs, 31 March 1978.

[17]Biggs interview with Gavin, 9 December 1968.

[18]Ibid.

[19]Gavin, *War and Peace,* p. 109.

[20]Ibid., p. 111.

[21]Biggs interview with Gavin, 9 December 1968.

[22]Ibid.

[23]Ibid.

[24]*Harper's,* April 1954.

[25]Gavin to Biggs, August 1967.

[26]Conversation between Gavin and staff in Germany, June 1953.

[27]Gavin to his staff officers in a July 1953 staff meeting.

[28]Ibid.

[29]Biggs interview with Gavin, 9 December 1968.

Chapter V

[1]*New York Times,* 13 January 1954, pp. 1–2.

[2]Biggs interview with Gavin, 26 December 1967.

[3]*New York Times,* 23 January 1954, pp. 1 and 5.

[4]Matthew Ridgway, *Soldier* (New York: Harper & Row, 1956), p. 274.

[5]Quoted in Arthur Schlesinger, *A Thousand Days* (Boston: Houghton-Mifflin, 1965), p. 310.

[6]Maxwell D. Taylor, *Swords and Plowshares* (New York: Norton, 1972), p. 156.

[7]Von Braun to Biggs, 22 July 1975.

[8]Biggs interview with Gavin, 26 December 1967.

[9]James M. Gavin, *War and Peace in the Space Age* (New York: Harper & Bros., 1956), p. 16.

[10]Ibid.

[11]Ibid., p. 124.

[12]Ibid., p. 12.

Chapter VI

[1]U.S., Congress, Senate, Preparedness Investigating Sub-

Committee of the Committee on Armed Forces, *Inquiry into Satellite and Missiles Program,* 80th Cong., 1st and 2d sess., 25 November 1957 through 23 January 1958, p. 481.

[2]Biggs interview with Gavin, 18 July 1972.

[3]Gavin to Biggs, 7 February 1977.

[4]*Inquiry into Satellite and Missiles Program,* p. 492.

[5]Ibid.

[6]Ibid., p. 502.

[7]Ibid.

[8]Biggs interview with John Eisenhower, 17 March 1973.

[9]Biggs interview with Gavin, 18 July 1972.

[10]Sutherland to Biggs, 22 August 1977.

[11]Westmoreland to Biggs, 27 May 1975.

[12]Biggs interview with Gavin, 18 July 1972; Gavin to Biggs, 26 March 1973.

[13]Sutherland to Biggs, 22 August 1977.

[14]Booth to Gavin, 3 September 1975.

[15]Gavin to Biggs, 7 February 1977.

[16]Biggs interview with Gavin, 24 February 1978.

[17]Biggs interview with Gavin, 19 June 1968.

[18]Ibid.

[19]Gavin to Biggs, 24 March 1958.

[20]Lemnitzer to Biggs, 28 February 1978.

[21]James M. Gavin, "The Tragic Mistakes and Bickering That Undermined U.S. Preparedness," *Life,* 4 August 1958, p. 75.

[22]Alexander de Seversky, *America: Too Young to Die* (New York: McGraw-Hill, 1961), p. 25.

[23]Biggs interview with Gavin, 4 August 1968.

[24]Gavin to Biggs, 24 February 1978.

Chapter VII

[1]Gavin to Biggs, 7 July 1973.

[2]Biggs interview with Gavin, 15 August 1978.

[3]Ibid.

[4]Ibid.

[5]Ibid.

[6]Jean Gavin, "When My Husband Retired from the Army," *Good Housekeeping,* June 1958.

[7]Biggs interview with Denninger, 18 August 1978.
[8]Herrmann to Biggs, 4 August 1978.
[9]Ibid.
[10]Gavin to Herrmann, 16 August 1978.
[11]Herrmann to Biggs, 4 August 1978.
[12]Ibid.
[13]Biggs interview with Magee, 1 April 1978.
[14]Biggs interview with Gavin, 14 August 1978.
[15]Herrmann to Biggs, 4 August 1978.
[16]Biggs interview with Magee, 1 April 1978.
[17]Herrmann to Biggs, 4 August 1978.
[18]Biggs interview with Rollins, 1 April 1978.
[19]James M. Gavin, *War and Peace in the Space Age* (New York: Harper & Bros., 1956), p. 284.
[20]Biggs interview with Gavin, 9 December 1968.
[21]*The Reporter,* 30 October 1958.
[22]Lyndon B. Johnson, *The Vantage Point* (New York: Popular Library, 1971), p. 278.

Chapter VIII

[1]Biggs interview with Gavin, 28 June 1972.
[2]Ibid.
[3]Ibid.
[4]James Reston, *New York Times,* 7 February 1961, p. 20.
[5]*Time,* 17 February 1961, p. 14.
[6]New York *Herald Tribune,* 9 February 1961.
[7]Biggs interview with Gavin, 28 June 1972.
[8]Ibid.
[9]Biggs interview with Collingwood, 12 February 1973.
[10]Biggs interview with Jean Gavin, 18 August 1972.
[11]Biggs interview with Gavin, 28 June 1972.
[12]Quoted in the *New York Times,* 17 June 1962, p. 26.
[13]Biggs interview with Gavin, 28 June 1972.
[14]Ibid.
[15]Ibid.
[16]Ibid.
[17]Ibid.
[18]Ibid.
[19]Ibid.

[20]Ibid.

Chapter IX

[1]Gavin to Biggs, 7 July 1978.
[2]Herrmann to Biggs, 4 August 1978.
[3]Ibid.
[4]Gavin to Biggs, 7 July 1978.
[5]Ibid.
[6]Gavin to Herrmann, 16 August 1978.
[7]*Nation's Business,* May 1978, pp. 42–48.
[8]Ibid.
[9]Herrmann to Biggs, 4 August 1978.
[10]Gavin to Biggs, 10 August 1978.
[11]Biggs interview with Rollins, 1 April 1978.
[12]Arthur D. Little Company, *Annual Report,* 1975.
[13]Arthur D. Little Company, *Annual Report,* 1976.
[14]Gavin to Barbara Gavin, 15 March 1964.

Chapter X

[1]Gavin, letter to *Harper's,* February 1966.
[2]Ridgway memorandum to Army Secretary Stevens, 17 May 1954.
[3]Biggs interview with Ridgway, 27 March 1970.
[4]Moos to Biggs, 2 April 1973.
[5]Biggs interview with Gavin, 14 August 1975.
[6]Quoted in William Manchester, *The Glory and the Dream* (Boston: Little, Brown & Co., 1974), p. 910.
[7]Biggs interview with Gavin, 14 August 1975.
[8]Ibid.
[9]Quoted in *New York Times,* 6 August 1964, p. 8.
[10]Biggs interview with Gavin, 14 August 1975.
[11]Quoted in Manchester, *The Glory and the Dream,* p. 1045.
[12]Gavin, letter to *Harper's.*
[13]*New York Times,* 17 January 1966, pp. 1 and 6.
[14]Gavin, letter to *Harper's.*
[15]Quoted in *New York Times,* 4 February 1966, p. 1.
[16]Biggs interview with Gavin, 14 August 1975.
[17]Quoted in David Halberstam, *The Best and the Brightest* (New York: Random House, 1972), p. 76.

[18]Seitz to Biggs, 24 April 1975.

[19]Biggs interview with McAuliffe, 28 April 1972.

[20]Gavin, interviewed on NBC's "Meet the Press," 12 November 1967.

[21]*Newsweek,* 3 January 1966.

[22]Biggs interview with Collins, 26 April 1973.

[23]U.S., Congress, Senate, Committee on Armed Services and the Subcommittee on Department of Defense of the Committee on Appropriations, *Supplemental Military Procurement and Construction Authorizations, Fiscal Year 1966,* 89th Cong., 2d sess., 20 January 1966, p. 41.

[24]U.S., Congress, Senate, Committee on Foreign Relations, *Supplemental Foreign Assistance, Fiscal Year 1966—Vietnam,* 89th Cong., 2d sess., 8 February 1966, pp. 226-325.

[25]U.S., Congress, Senate, Committee on Foreign Relations, *Conflicts Between United States Capabilities and Foreign Commitments,* 90th Cong., 1st sess., 21 February 1967.

[26]Biggs interview with Gavin, 14 August 1968.

[27]Ridgway to Biggs, 18 January 1976.

[28]Biggs, et al. interview with Gavin, 9 February 1978.

[29]Biggs interview with Gavin, 14 August 1968.

[30]Christopher Lydon and Ted Dully, "General Gavin Steps Front and Center," *Boston Globe,* 10 September 1967.

[31]Ibid.

[32]Quoted in *U.S. News and World Report,* 20 November 1967.

[33]Herrmann to Biggs, 4 August 1978.

[34]Marquis Childs, "The Mini Boom for Gavin," *Middletown Press,* August 1967.

[35]Lewis Chester, Godfrey Hodgson, and Bruce Page, *An American Melodrama—The Presidential Campaign of 1968* (New York: Viking Press, 1969), pp. 65-66.

[36]Biggs interview with Gavin, 14 August 1975.

[37]McGovern to Biggs, 30 April 1975.

[38]Biggs interview with Gavin, 14 August 1975.

Chapter XI

[1]Biggs interview with Gavin, 9 December 1968.
[2]Ibid.

[3]Ibid.

[4]Gavin to Biggs, 1 March 1977.

[5]Biggs interview with Gavin, 9 December 1968.

[6]Ibid.

[7]Biggs interview with Gavin, 8 December 1978.

[8]*Newsweek,* 10 January 1958.

[9]James M. Gavin, "National Priorities in an Age of Change" (speech delivered at the Palmer House, Chicago, 19 April 1968).

[10]James M. Gavin, "National Priorities and National Policies" (speech delivered at Dartmouth College, Hanover, New Hampshire, 25 January 1968).

[11]James M. Gavin with Arthur T. Hadley, *Crisis Now* (New York: Random House, 1968), p. 99.

[12]Gavin to Biggs, 12 April 1967.

[13]James M. Gavin, "Perspectives and Prospects in Space" (speech delivered to the American Institute of Aeronautics and Astronautics, Boston, Massachusetts, 1 December 1966).

[14]Biggs interview with Aileen Gavin, October 1977.

Index